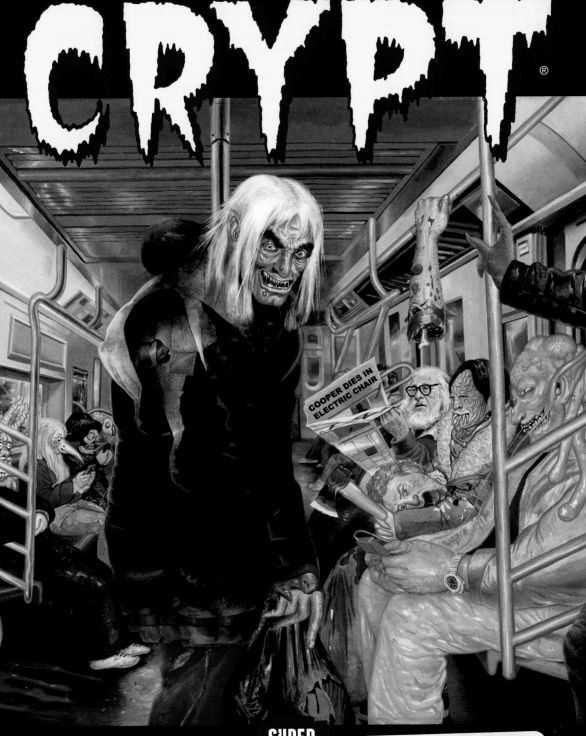

TALES
FROM THE
CRYPT ®

COOPER DIES IN
ELECTRIC CHAIR

GRAPHIC NOVELS AVAILABLE FROM SUPER GENIUS

NEIL GAIMAN'S
Lady JUSTICE
THE COMPLETE COMICS
VOLUME ONE

NEIL GAIMAN'S
LADY JUSTICE
Volume One

NEIL GAIMAN'S
Lady JUSTICE

NEIL GAIMAN'S
LADY JUSTICE
Volume Two

NEIL GAIMAN'S
TEKNOPHAGE
THE COMPLETE COMICS
VOLUME ONE

NEIL GAIMAN'S
TEKNOPHAGE
Volume One

NEIL GAIMAN'S
TEKNOPHAGE
THE COMPLETE COMICS
VOLUME TWO

NEIL GAIMAN'S
TEKNOPHAGE
Volume Two

NEIL GAIMAN'S
MR HERO
THE NEWMATIC MAN
THE COMPLETE COMICS
VOLUME ONE

NEIL GAIMAN'S
MR. HERO
Volume One

NEIL GAIMAN'S
MR HERO
THE NEWMATIC MAN
THE COMPLETE COMICS
VOLUME TWO

NEIL GAIMAN'S
MR. HERO
Volume Two

JESSICA ABEL
TRISH TRASH
ROLLERGIRL OF MARS

TRISH TRASH #1
Rollergirl of Mars
By Jessica Abel

JESSICA ABEL
TRISH TRASH
ROLLERGIRL OF MARS

TRISH TRASH #2
Rollergirl of Mars
By Jessica Abel

THE CHILDREN OF
CAPTAIN GRANT

THE CHILDREN OF
CAPTAIN GRANT
By Jules Verne
Adapted by Alexis Nesme

THE Wendy PROJECT
OSBORNE FISH

THE WENDY PROJECT
By Melissa Jane Osborne
& Veronica Fish

NEIL GAIMAN'S LADY JUSTICE, NEIL GAIMAN'S TEKNOPHAGE, NEIL GAIMAN'S MR. HERO, THE CHILDREN OF CAPTAIN GRANT, TRISH TRASH, and THE WENDY PROJECT graphic novels are available at booksellers everywhere. NEIL GAIMAN'S LADY JUSTICE Volume One & Two, NEIL GAIMAN'S TEKNOPHAGE Volume One & Two, and NEI GAIMAN'S MR. HERO Volume One are $14.99 each in paperback, and $24.99 each in hardcover. THE CHILDREN OF CAPTAIN GRAN is $14.99 in paperback, and $19.99 in hardcover. TRISH TRASH is $14.99 in hardcover only. THE WENDY PROJECT is $12.99 in paperback only. You may also order online at supergeniuscomics.com. Or call 1-800-886-1223, Monday through Friday, 9 – 5 EST MC, Visa, and AmEx accepted. To order by mail, please add $5.0 for postage and handling for first book ordered, $1.00 for each additional book and make check payable to NBM Publishing. Send to: Super Genius, 160 Broadway, Suite 700, East Wing, New York, NY 10038.

NEIL GAIMAN'S LADY JUSTICE, NEIL GAIMAN'S TEKNOPHAGE, NEIL GAIMAN'S MR. HERO, THE CHILDREN OF CAPTAIN GRANT, TRISH TRASH, and THE WENDY PROJECT graphic novels are also available digitally wherever e-books are sold.

SUPERGENIUSCOMICS.COM

TALES FROM THE CRYPT®

Danica Davidson

CHRISTINA BLANCH
DANICA DAVIDSON
DAVID ANTHONY KRAFT & ONRIE KOMPAN
SCOTT LOBDELL
STEFAN PETRUCHA
Writers

KYLE BAKER
BOB CAMP
DEAN HASPIEL
RUSS HEATH
MIRAN KIM
STEVE MANNION
JOHN McCREA
JOLYON YATES
Artists

BERNIE WRIGHTSON
Writer/Artist

"Creep' Reading!
Dr. Christy P.

SUPER GENIUS

TALES FROM THE CRYPT®

"STAKE OUT!"
Bernie Wrightson
Writer & Artist
Laurie E. Smith
Colorist
Tom Orzechowski
Letterer

"DIE-VESTMENT!"
Stefan Petrucha
Writer
Jolyon Yates
Artist
JayJay Jackson
Colorist

"ZOMBIE BANK"
David Anthony Kraft &
Onrie Kompan
Writers
Miran Kim
Artist & Colorist
Tom Orzechowski
Letterer

"THE WEREWOLF OF WALL STREET"
Scott Lobdell
Writer
John McCrea
Artist
Dee Cunniffe
Colorist
Tom Orzechowski
Letterer

"PICTURE PERFECT"
Danica Davidson
Writer
Jolyon Yates
Artist
JayJay Jackson
Colorist
Tom Orzechowski
Letterer

"UNDERTOW"
Christina Blanch
Writer
Miran Kim
Artist & Colorist
Tom Orzechowski
Letterer

"FEED IT!"
Bernie Wrightson
Writer & Artist
(The Vault-Keeper by
Jolyon Yates)
Laurie E. Smith
Colorist
Tom Orzechowski
Letterer

"LEATHER OR NOT"
Christina Blanch
Writer
Miran Kim
Artist & Colorist
Tom Orzechowski
Letterer

AN ENTERTAINING EC COMIC

Miran Kim (page 1) · Jolyon Yates (Pages 9, 46) · Bob Camp (Page 10) · Dean Haspiel (Page 27) · Russ Heath (Page 28) · Kyle Baker (Page 61) · Steve Mannion (Front Cover, Page 62)

Cover Artists

Dawn Guzzo – Design & Production
Dorothy Crouch, Cathy Gaines Mifsud, Corey Mifsud (corey@ECcomics.com) – Special Thanks
Michael Catron, Liz Wrightson – Extra Special Thanks
Jeff Whitman – Assistant Managing Editor
Jim Salicrup
Editor-in-Chief

ISBN: 978-1-62991-460-2 Paperback Edition
ISBN: 978-1-62991-461-9 Hardcover Edition

Super Genius books may be purchased for business or promotional use.
For information on bulk purchases please contact Macmillan Corporate and Premium Sales Department at (800) 221-7945 x5442.

SUPER GENIUS

Super Genius is an imprint of Papercutz.

Printed in China.
December 2017

Distributed by Macmillan
First Printing

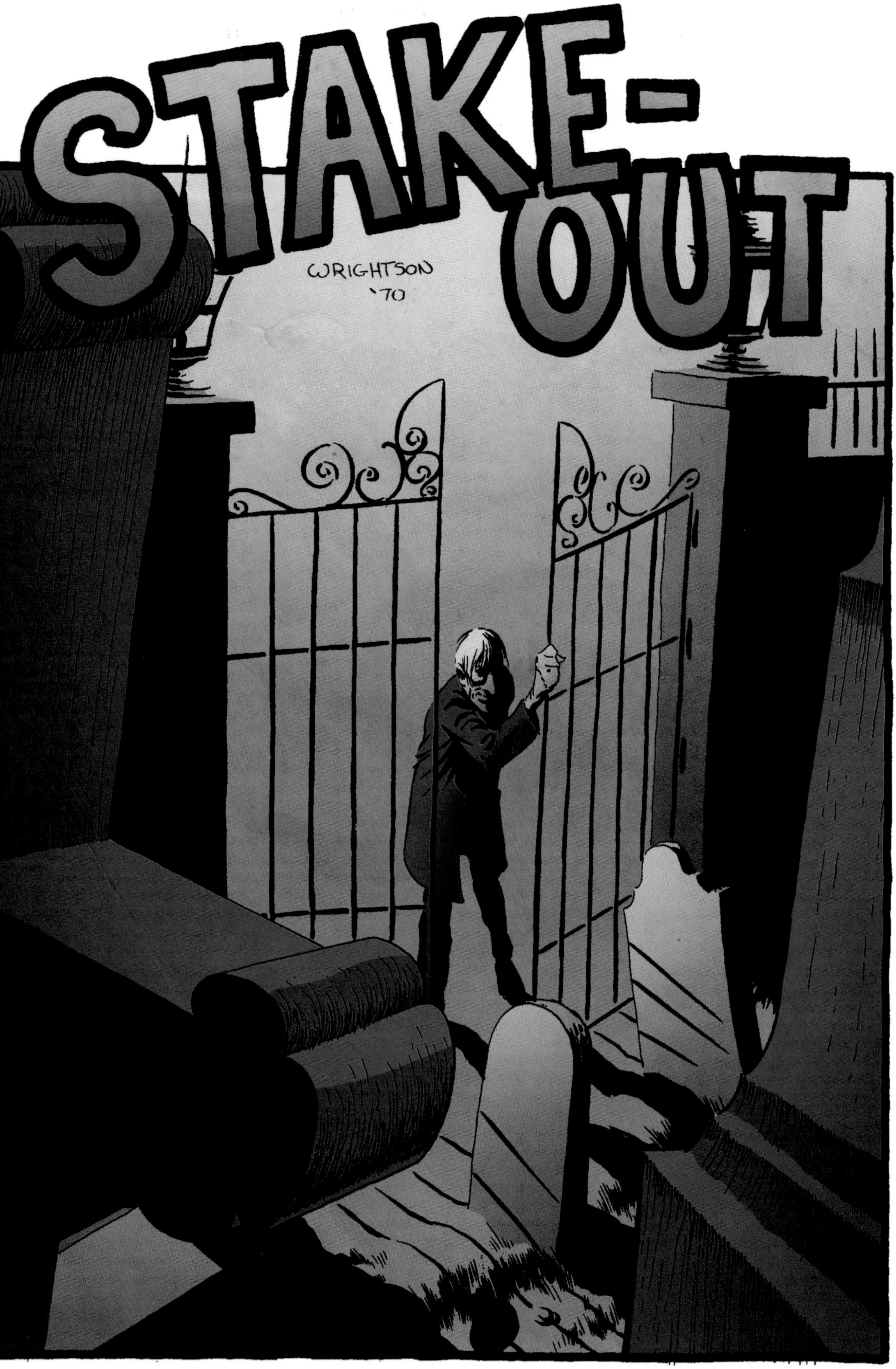
STAKE-OUT
WRIGHTSON '70

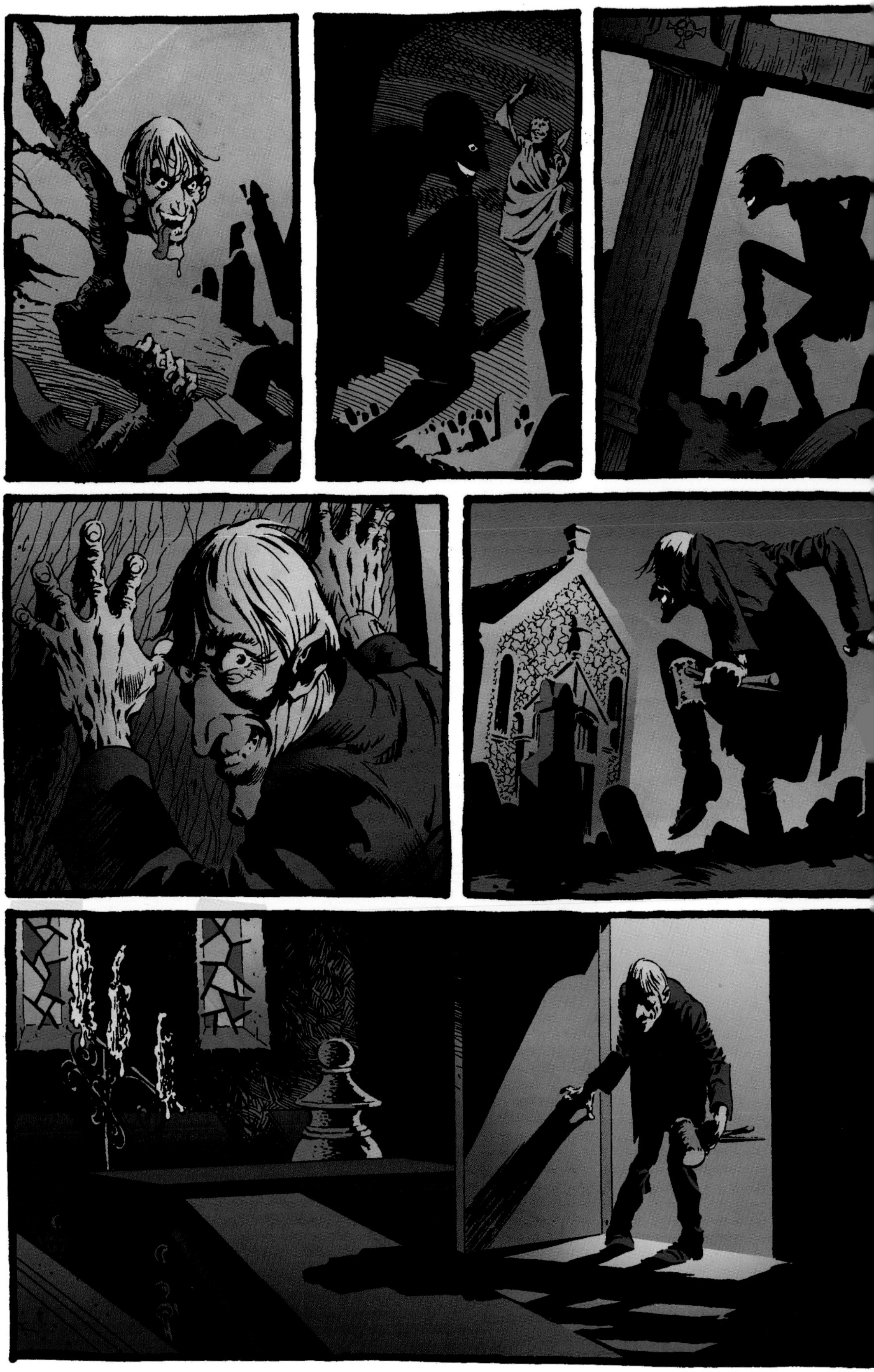

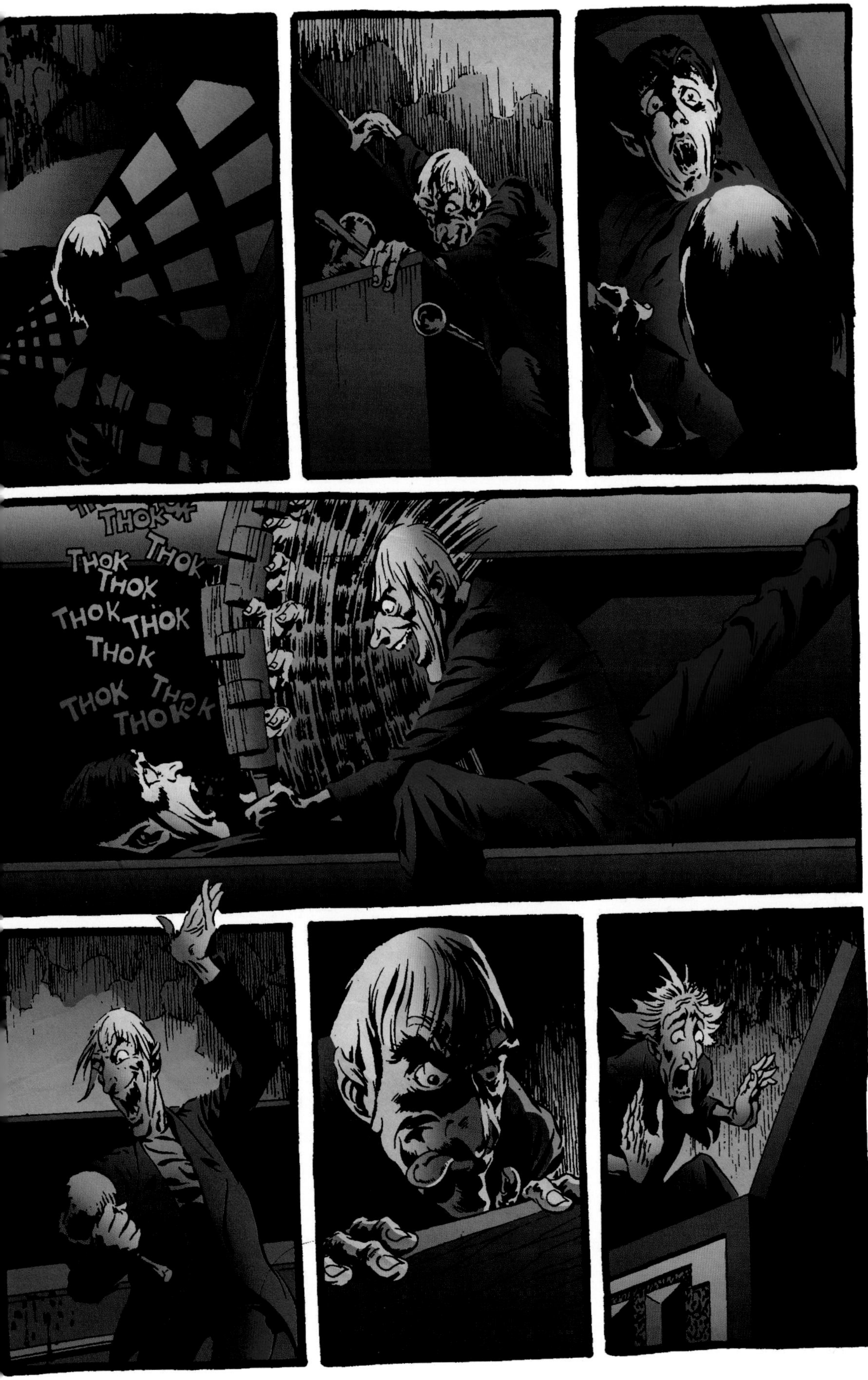
THOK
THOK
THOK
THOK
THOK
THOK
THOK
THOK
THOK
THOK

GOOD LORD!! THAT WAS FREDDY AGAIN!
WHY CAN'T THEY JUST LET US REST IN PEACE?
NO MATTER WHERE WE GO, SOMEBODY ALWAYS MANAGES TO DIG US UP!!
THE HAUNT OF

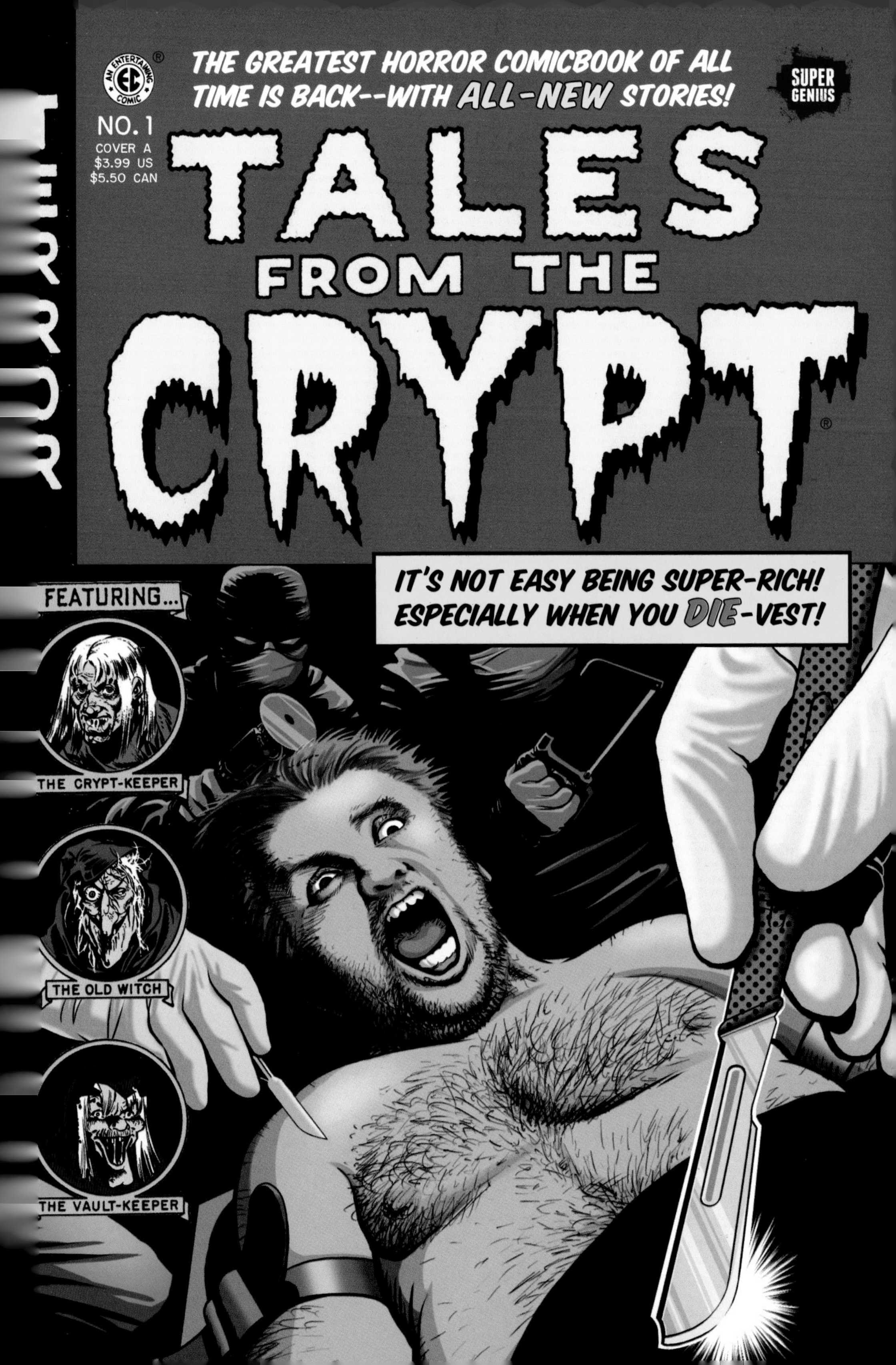
THE GREATEST HORROR COMICBOOK OF ALL TIME IS BACK--WITH ALL-NEW STORIES!
SUPER GENIUS
AN ENTERTAINING COMIC EC
NO. 1
COVER A
$3.99 US
$5.50 CAN
TALES FROM THE CRYPT
TERROR
IT'S NOT EASY BEING SUPER-RICH! ESPECIALLY WHEN YOU DIE-VEST!
FEATURING...
THE CRYPT-KEEPER
THE OLD WITCH
THE VAULT-KEEPER

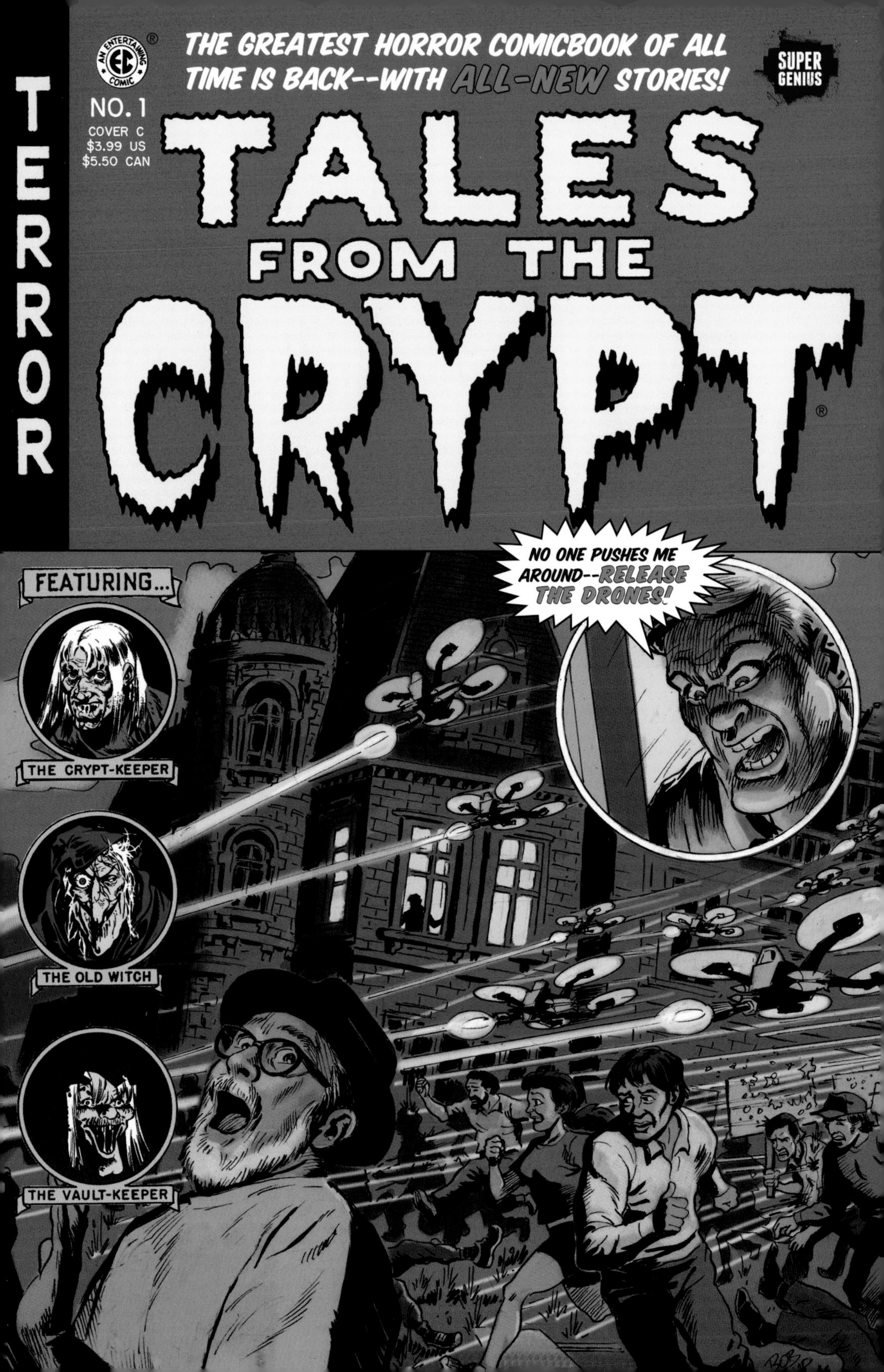

AN ENTERTAINING COMIC EC
THE GREATEST HORROR COMICBOOK OF ALL TIME IS BACK--WITH ALL-NEW STORIES!
SUPER GENIUS
NO. 1
COVER C
$3.99 US
$5.50 CAN
TERROR
TALES FROM THE CRYPT
FEATURING...
THE CRYPT-KEEPER
THE OLD WITCH
THE VAULT-KEEPER
NO ONE PUSHES ME AROUND--RELEASE THE DRONES!

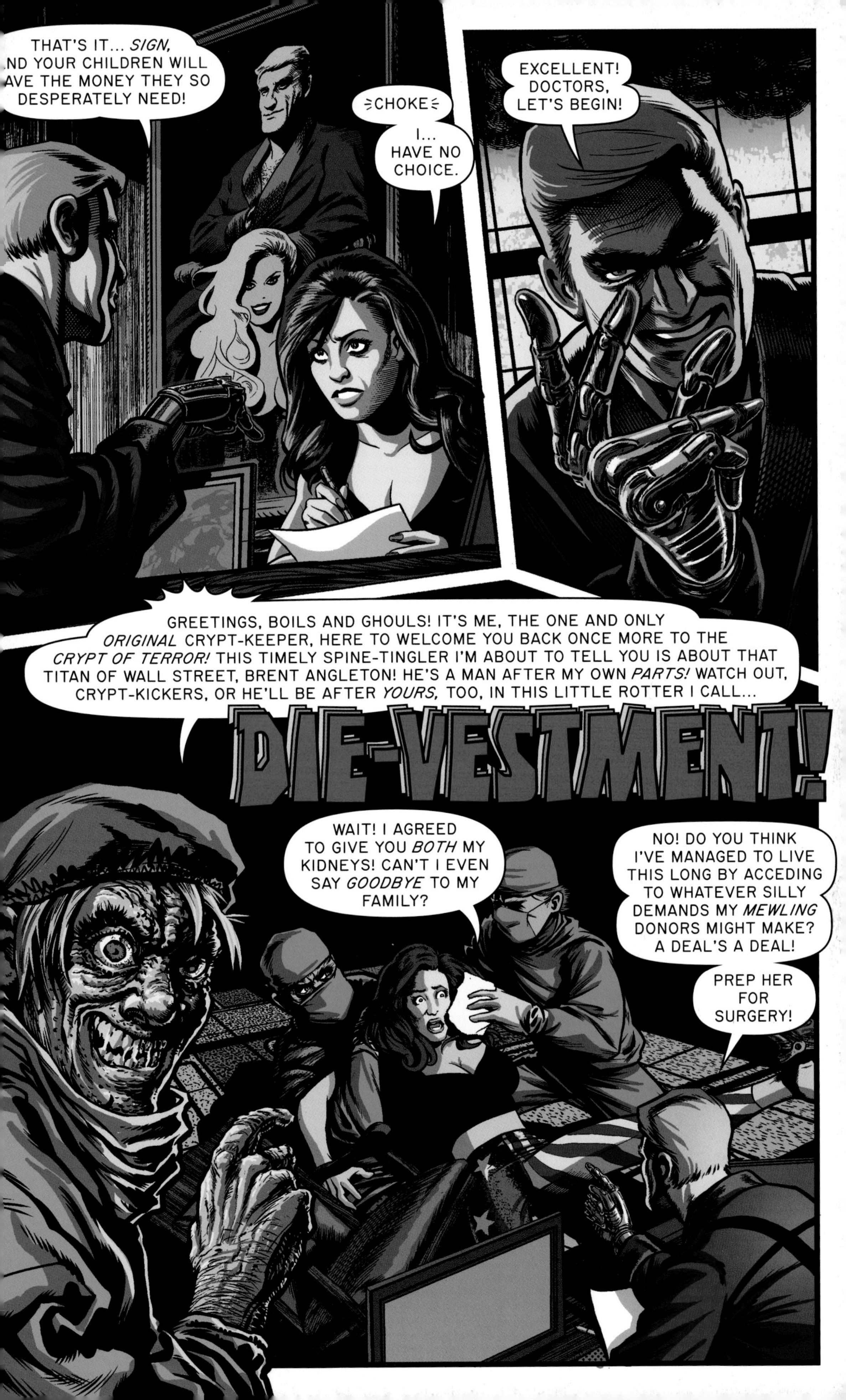

THAT'S IT... *SIGN,* ND YOUR CHILDREN WILL AVE THE MONEY THEY SO DESPERATELY NEED!
CHOKE
I... HAVE NO CHOICE.
EXCELLENT! DOCTORS, LET'S BEGIN!
GREETINGS, BOILS AND GHOULS! IT'S ME, THE ONE AND ONLY *ORIGINAL* CRYPT-KEEPER, HERE TO WELCOME YOU BACK ONCE MORE TO THE *CRYPT OF TERROR!* THIS TIMELY SPINE-TINGLER I'M ABOUT TO TELL YOU IS ABOUT THAT TITAN OF WALL STREET, BRENT ANGLETON! HE'S A MAN AFTER MY OWN *PARTS!* WATCH OUT, CRYPT-KICKERS, OR HE'LL BE AFTER *YOURS,* TOO, IN THIS LITTLE ROTTER I CALL...
DIE-VESTMENT!
WAIT! I AGREED TO GIVE YOU *BOTH* MY KIDNEYS! CAN'T I EVEN SAY *GOODBYE* TO MY FAMILY?
NO! DO YOU THINK I'VE MANAGED TO LIVE THIS LONG BY ACCEDING TO WHATEVER SILLY DEMANDS MY *MEWLING* DONORS MIGHT MAKE? A DEAL'S A DEAL!
PREP HER FOR SURGERY!

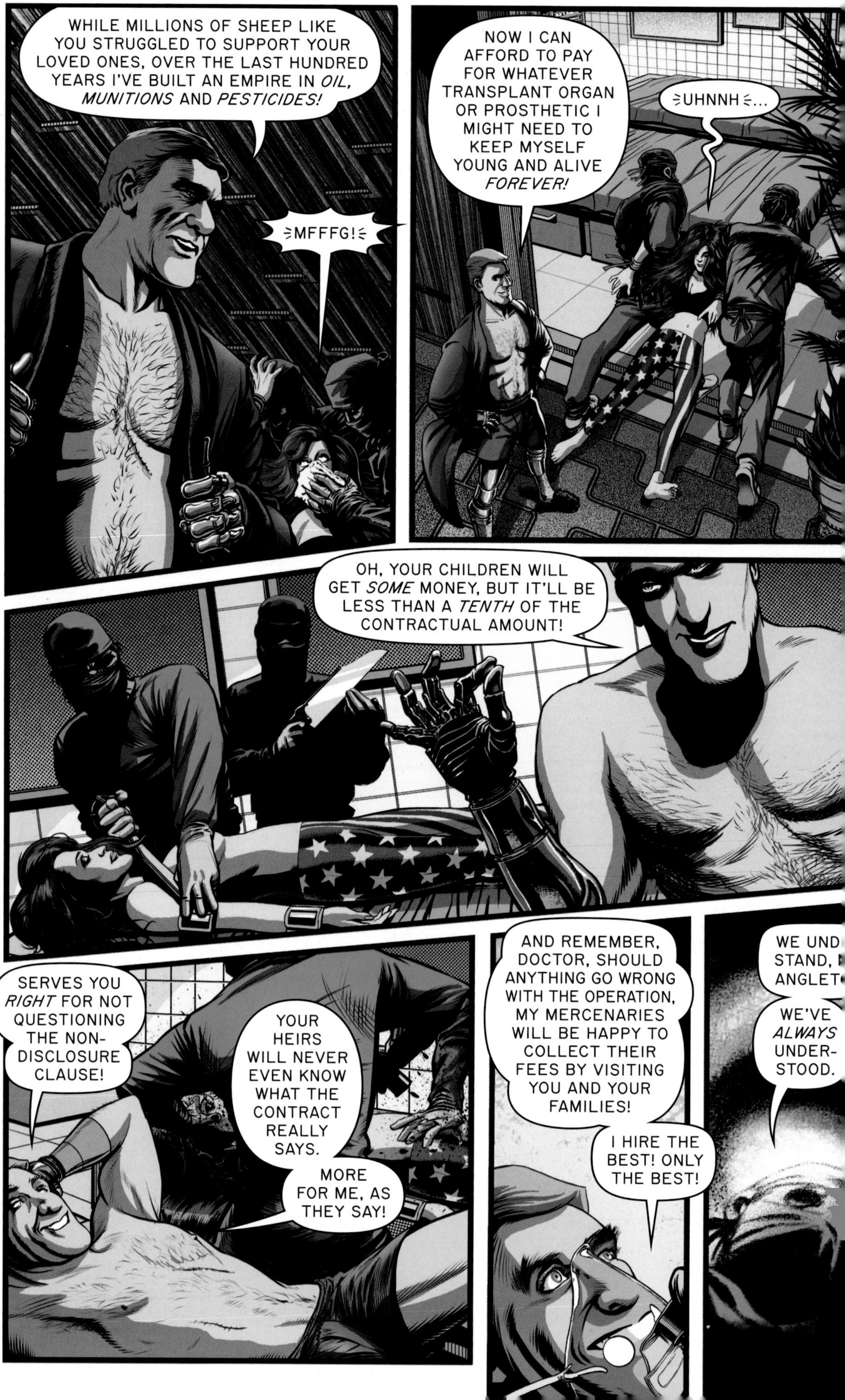

WHILE MILLIONS OF SHEEP LIKE YOU STRUGGLED TO SUPPORT YOUR LOVED ONES, OVER THE LAST HUNDRED YEARS I'VE BUILT AN EMPIRE IN *OIL, MUNITIONS* AND *PESTICIDES!*
MFFFG!
NOW I CAN AFFORD TO PAY FOR WHATEVER TRANSPLANT ORGAN OR PROSTHETIC I MIGHT NEED TO KEEP MYSELF YOUNG AND ALIVE *FOREVER!*
UHNNH...
OH, YOUR CHILDREN WILL GET *SOME* MONEY, BUT IT'LL BE LESS THAN A *TENTH* OF THE CONTRACTUAL AMOUNT!
SERVES YOU *RIGHT* FOR NOT QUESTIONING THE NON-DISCLOSURE CLAUSE!
YOUR HEIRS WILL NEVER EVEN KNOW WHAT THE CONTRACT REALLY SAYS.
MORE FOR ME, AS THEY SAY!
AND REMEMBER, DOCTOR, SHOULD ANYTHING GO WRONG WITH THE OPERATION, MY MERCENARIES WILL BE HAPPY TO COLLECT THEIR FEES BY VISITING YOU AND YOUR FAMILIES!
I HIRE THE BEST! ONLY THE BEST!
WE UND STAND, ANGLET
WE'VE *ALWAYS* UNDER-STOOD.

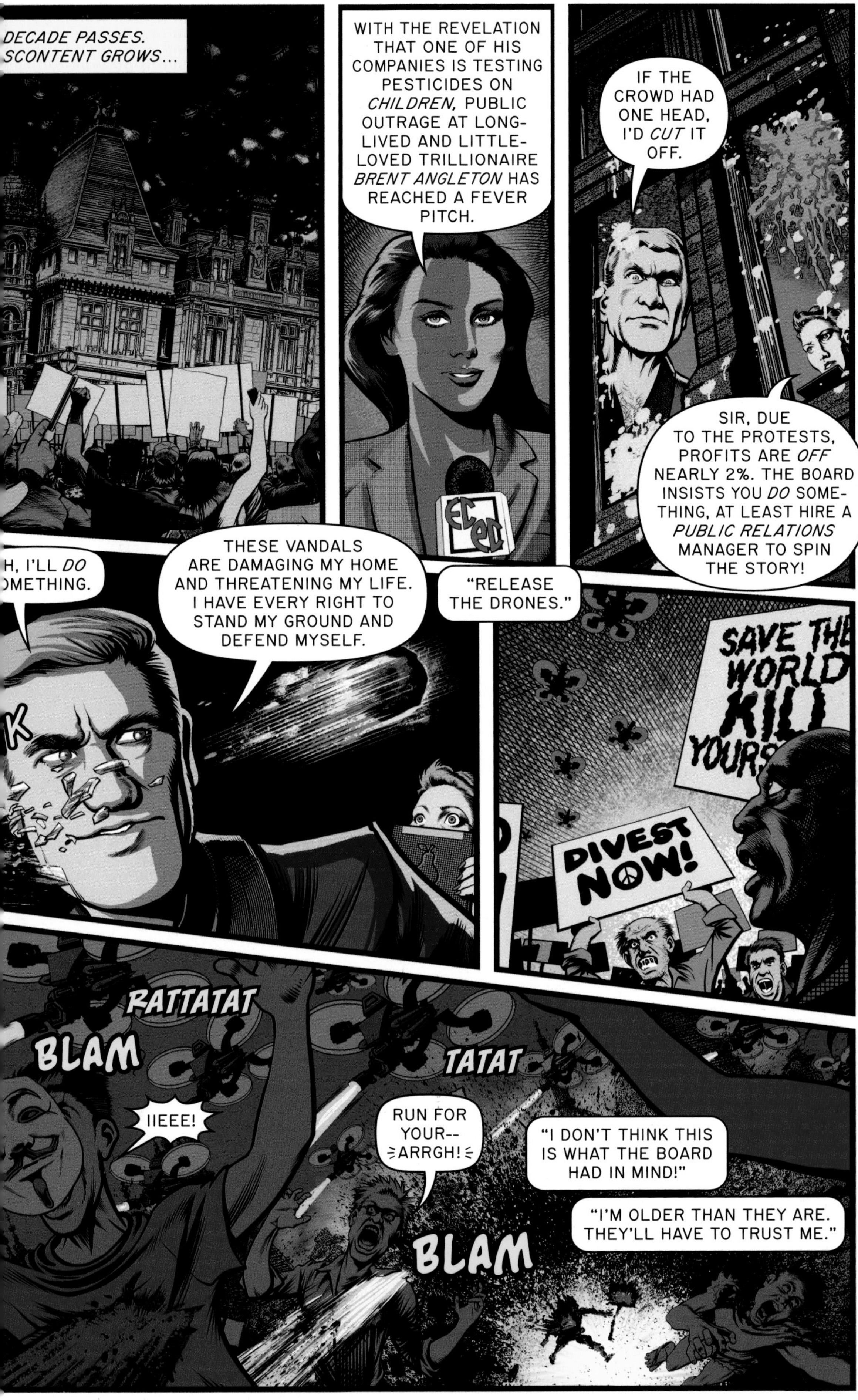
DECADE PASSES.
SCONTENT GROWS...
WITH THE REVELATION THAT ONE OF HIS COMPANIES IS TESTING PESTICIDES ON *CHILDREN,* PUBLIC OUTRAGE AT LONG-LIVED AND LITTLE-LOVED TRILLIONAIRE *BRENT ANGLETON* HAS REACHED A FEVER PITCH.
IF THE CROWD HAD ONE HEAD, I'D *CUT* IT OFF.
SIR, DUE TO THE PROTESTS, PROFITS ARE *OFF* NEARLY 2%. THE BOARD INSISTS YOU *DO* SOME-THING, AT LEAST HIRE A *PUBLIC RELATIONS* MANAGER TO SPIN THE STORY!
H, I'LL *DO* OMETHING.
THESE VANDALS ARE DAMAGING MY HOME AND THREATENING MY LIFE. I HAVE EVERY RIGHT TO STAND MY GROUND AND DEFEND MYSELF.
"RELEASE THE DRONES."
SAVE THE WORLD KILL YOURS
DIVEST NOW!
RATTATAT
BLAM
TATAT
IIEEE!
RUN FOR YOUR-- ARRGH!
"I DON'T THINK THIS IS WHAT THE BOARD HAD IN MIND!"
"I'M OLDER THAN THEY ARE. THEY'LL HAVE TO TRUST ME."
BLAM

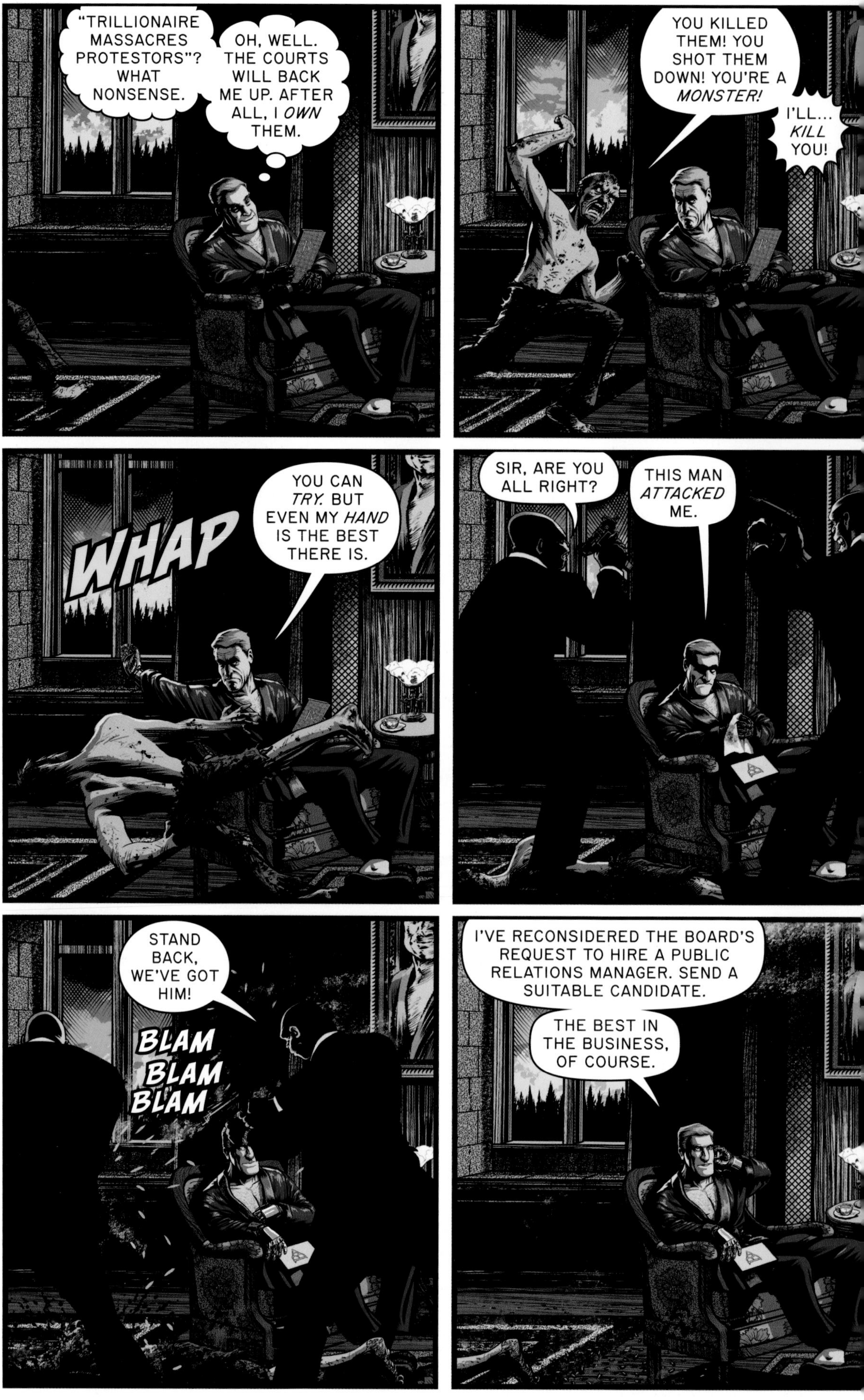
"TRILLIONAIRE MASSACRES PROTESTORS"? WHAT NONSENSE.
OH, WELL. THE COURTS WILL BACK ME UP. AFTER ALL, I *OWN* THEM.
YOU KILLED THEM! YOU SHOT THEM DOWN! YOU'RE A *MONSTER!*
I'LL... *KILL* YOU!
WHAP
YOU CAN *TRY.* BUT EVEN MY *HAND* IS THE BEST THERE IS.
SIR, ARE YOU ALL RIGHT?
THIS MAN *ATTACKED* ME.
STAND BACK, WE'VE GOT HIM!
BLAM BLAM BLAM
I'VE RECONSIDERED THE BOARD'S REQUEST TO HIRE A PUBLIC RELATIONS MANAGER. SEND A SUITABLE CANDIDATE.
THE BEST IN THE BUSINESS, OF COURSE.

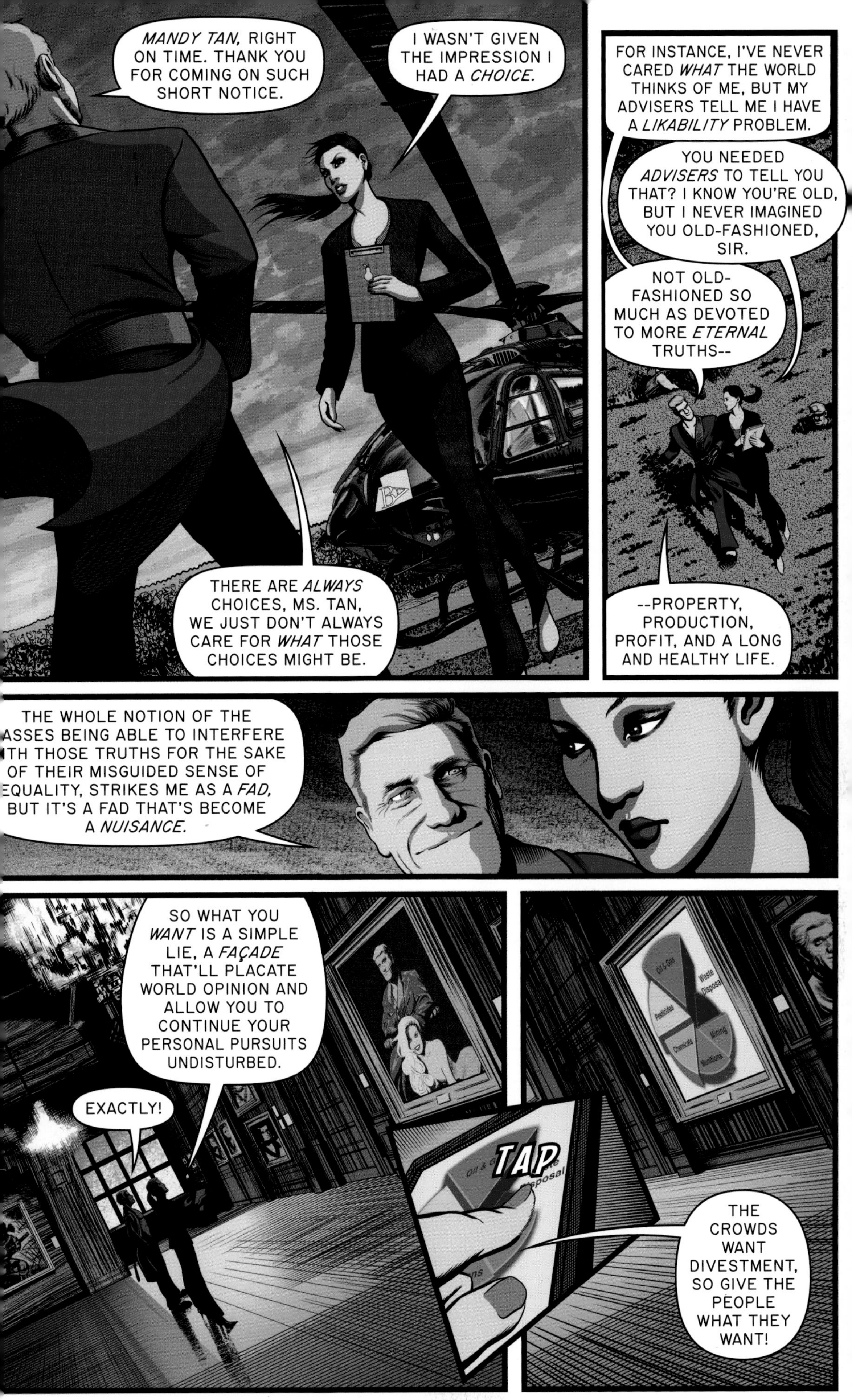
MANDY TAN, RIGHT ON TIME. THANK YOU FOR COMING ON SUCH SHORT NOTICE.
I WASN'T GIVEN THE IMPRESSION I HAD A CHOICE.
THERE ARE ALWAYS CHOICES, MS. TAN, WE JUST DON'T ALWAYS CARE FOR WHAT THOSE CHOICES MIGHT BE.
FOR INSTANCE, I'VE NEVER CARED WHAT THE WORLD THINKS OF ME, BUT MY ADVISERS TELL ME I HAVE A LIKABILITY PROBLEM.
YOU NEEDED ADVISERS TO TELL YOU THAT? I KNOW YOU'RE OLD, BUT I NEVER IMAGINED YOU OLD-FASHIONED, SIR.
NOT OLD-FASHIONED SO MUCH AS DEVOTED TO MORE ETERNAL TRUTHS--
--PROPERTY, PRODUCTION, PROFIT, AND A LONG AND HEALTHY LIFE.
THE WHOLE NOTION OF THE ASSES BEING ABLE TO INTERFERE TH THOSE TRUTHS FOR THE SAKE OF THEIR MISGUIDED SENSE OF QUALITY, STRIKES ME AS A FAD, BUT IT'S A FAD THAT'S BECOME A NUISANCE.
SO WHAT YOU WANT IS A SIMPLE LIE, A FAÇADE THAT'LL PLACATE WORLD OPINION AND ALLOW YOU TO CONTINUE YOUR PERSONAL PURSUITS UNDISTURBED.
EXACTLY!
Oil & Gas
Waste Disposal
Pesticides
Chemicals
Mining
Munitions
TAP
THE CROWDS WANT DIVESTMENT, SO GIVE THE PEOPLE WHAT THEY WANT!

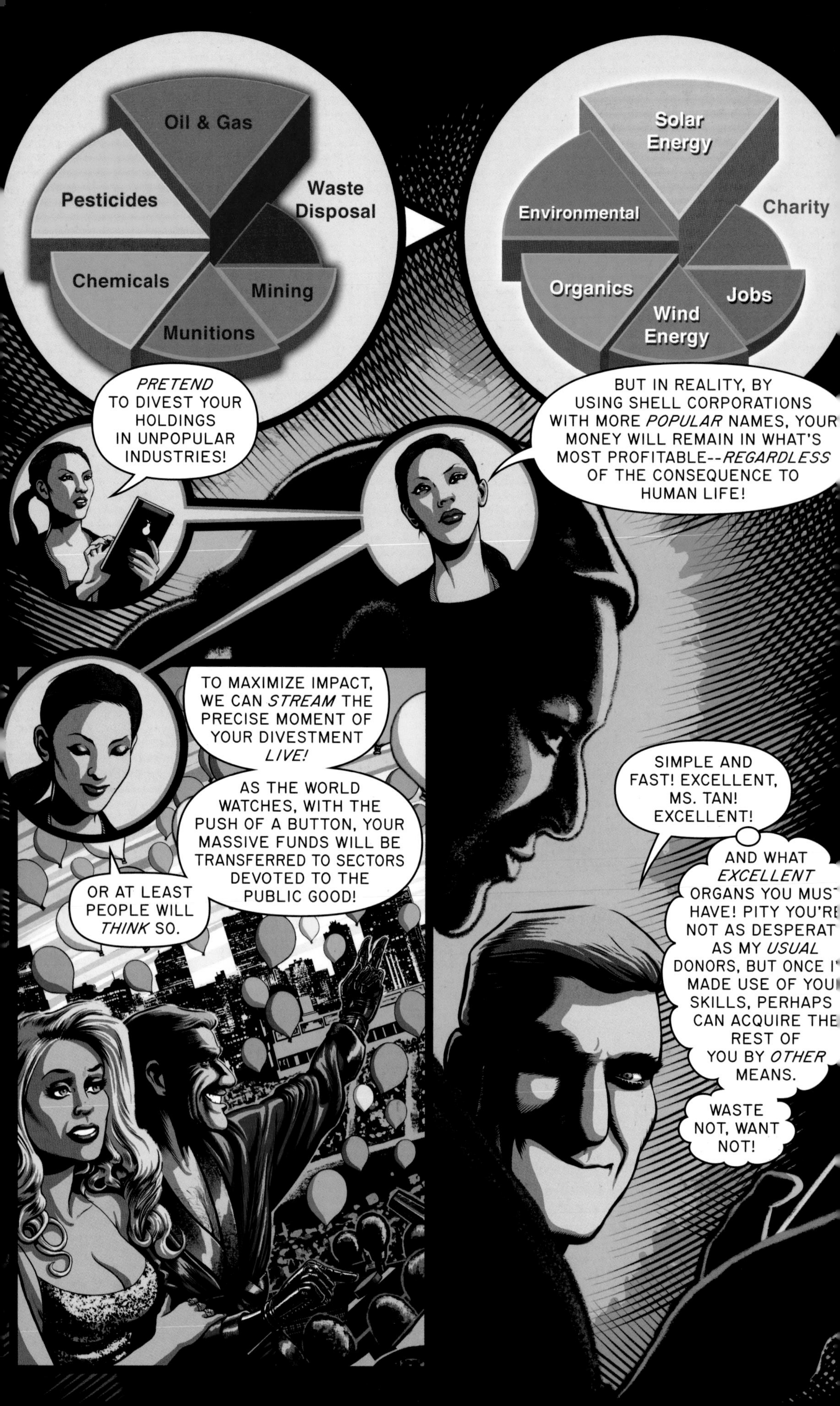
Oil & Gas
Pesticides
Waste Disposal
Chemicals
Mining
Munitions
Solar Energy
Environmental
Charity
Organics
Jobs
Wind Energy
PRETEND TO DIVEST YOUR HOLDINGS IN UNPOPULAR INDUSTRIES!
BUT IN REALITY, BY USING SHELL CORPORATIONS WITH MORE POPULAR NAMES, YOUR MONEY WILL REMAIN IN WHAT'S MOST PROFITABLE--REGARDLESS OF THE CONSEQUENCE TO HUMAN LIFE!
TO MAXIMIZE IMPACT, WE CAN STREAM THE PRECISE MOMENT OF YOUR DIVESTMENT LIVE!
AS THE WORLD WATCHES, WITH THE PUSH OF A BUTTON, YOUR MASSIVE FUNDS WILL BE TRANSFERRED TO SECTORS DEVOTED TO THE PUBLIC GOOD!
OR AT LEAST PEOPLE WILL THINK SO.
SIMPLE AND FAST! EXCELLENT, MS. TAN! EXCELLENT!
AND WHAT EXCELLENT ORGANS YOU MUST HAVE! PITY YOU'RE NOT AS DESPERATE AS MY USUAL DONORS, BUT ONCE I'VE MADE USE OF YOUR SKILLS, PERHAPS I CAN ACQUIRE THE REST OF YOU BY OTHER MEANS.
WASTE NOT, WANT NOT!

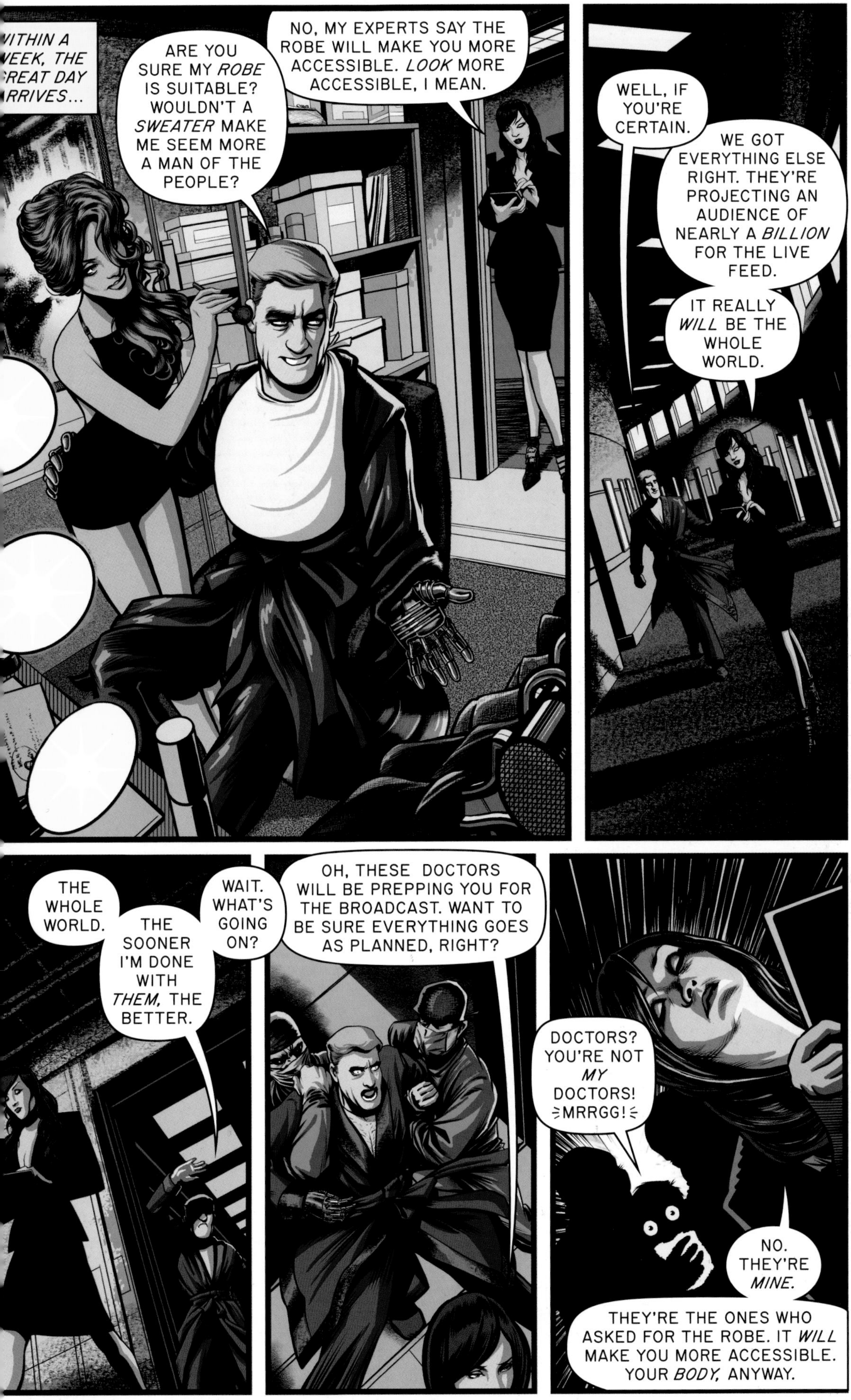

WITHIN A WEEK, THE GREAT DAY ARRIVES...
ARE YOU SURE MY *ROBE* IS SUITABLE? WOULDN'T A *SWEATER* MAKE ME SEEM MORE A MAN OF THE PEOPLE?
NO, MY EXPERTS SAY THE ROBE WILL MAKE YOU MORE ACCESSIBLE. *LOOK* MORE ACCESSIBLE, I MEAN.
WELL, IF YOU'RE CERTAIN.
WE GOT EVERYTHING ELSE RIGHT. THEY'RE PROJECTING AN AUDIENCE OF NEARLY A *BILLION* FOR THE LIVE FEED.
IT REALLY *WILL* BE THE WHOLE WORLD.
THE WHOLE WORLD.
THE SOONER I'M DONE WITH *THEM,* THE BETTER.
WAIT. WHAT'S GOING ON?
OH, THESE DOCTORS WILL BE PREPPING YOU FOR THE BROADCAST. WANT TO BE SURE EVERYTHING GOES AS PLANNED, RIGHT?
DOCTORS? YOU'RE NOT *MY* DOCTORS! MRRGG!
NO. THEY'RE *MINE.*
THEY'RE THE ONES WHO ASKED FOR THE ROBE. IT *WILL* MAKE YOU MORE ACCESSIBLE. YOUR *BODY,* ANYWAY.

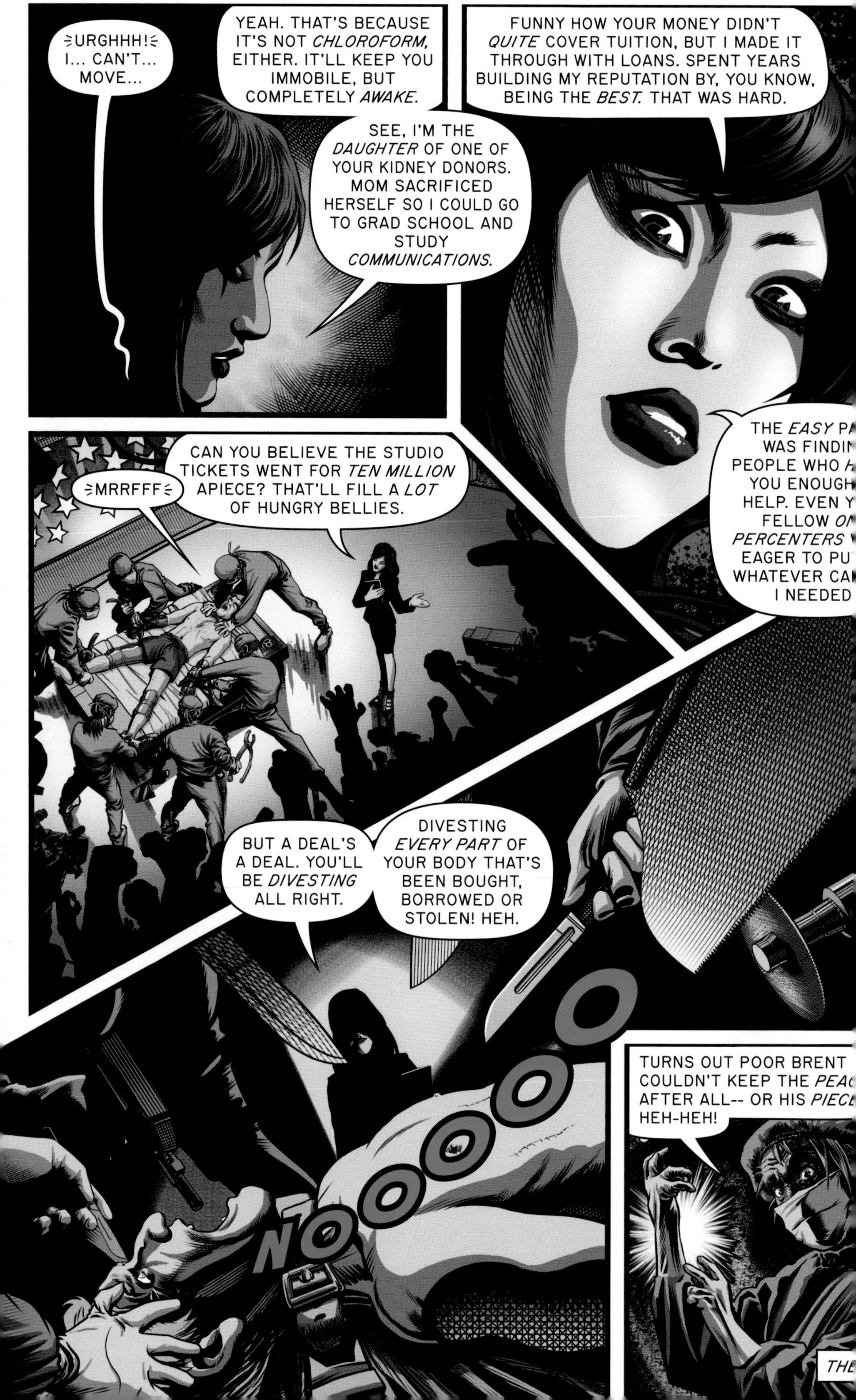

URGHHH! I... CAN'T... MOVE...
YEAH. THAT'S BECAUSE IT'S NOT *CHLOROFORM,* EITHER. IT'LL KEEP YOU IMMOBILE, BUT COMPLETELY *AWAKE.*
SEE, I'M THE *DAUGHTER* OF ONE OF YOUR KIDNEY DONORS. MOM SACRIFICED HERSELF SO I COULD GO TO GRAD SCHOOL AND STUDY *COMMUNICATIONS.*
FUNNY HOW YOUR MONEY DIDN'T *QUITE* COVER TUITION, BUT I MADE IT THROUGH WITH LOANS. SPENT YEARS BUILDING MY REPUTATION BY, YOU KNOW, BEING THE *BEST.* THAT WAS HARD.
THE *EASY* P WAS FINDI PEOPLE WHO YOU ENOUGH HELP. EVEN Y FELLOW *O* *PERCENTERS* EAGER TO PU WHATEVER CA I NEEDED
CAN YOU BELIEVE THE STUDIO TICKETS WENT FOR *TEN MILLION* APIECE? THAT'LL FILL A *LOT* OF HUNGRY BELLIES.
MRRFFF
BUT A DEAL'S A DEAL. YOU'LL BE *DIVESTING* ALL RIGHT.
DIVESTING *EVERY PART* OF YOUR BODY THAT'S BEEN BOUGHT, BORROWED OR STOLEN! HEH.
NOOOOOOOO
TURNS OUT POOR BRENT COULDN'T KEEP THE *PEA* AFTER ALL-- OR HIS *PIEC* HEH-HEH!

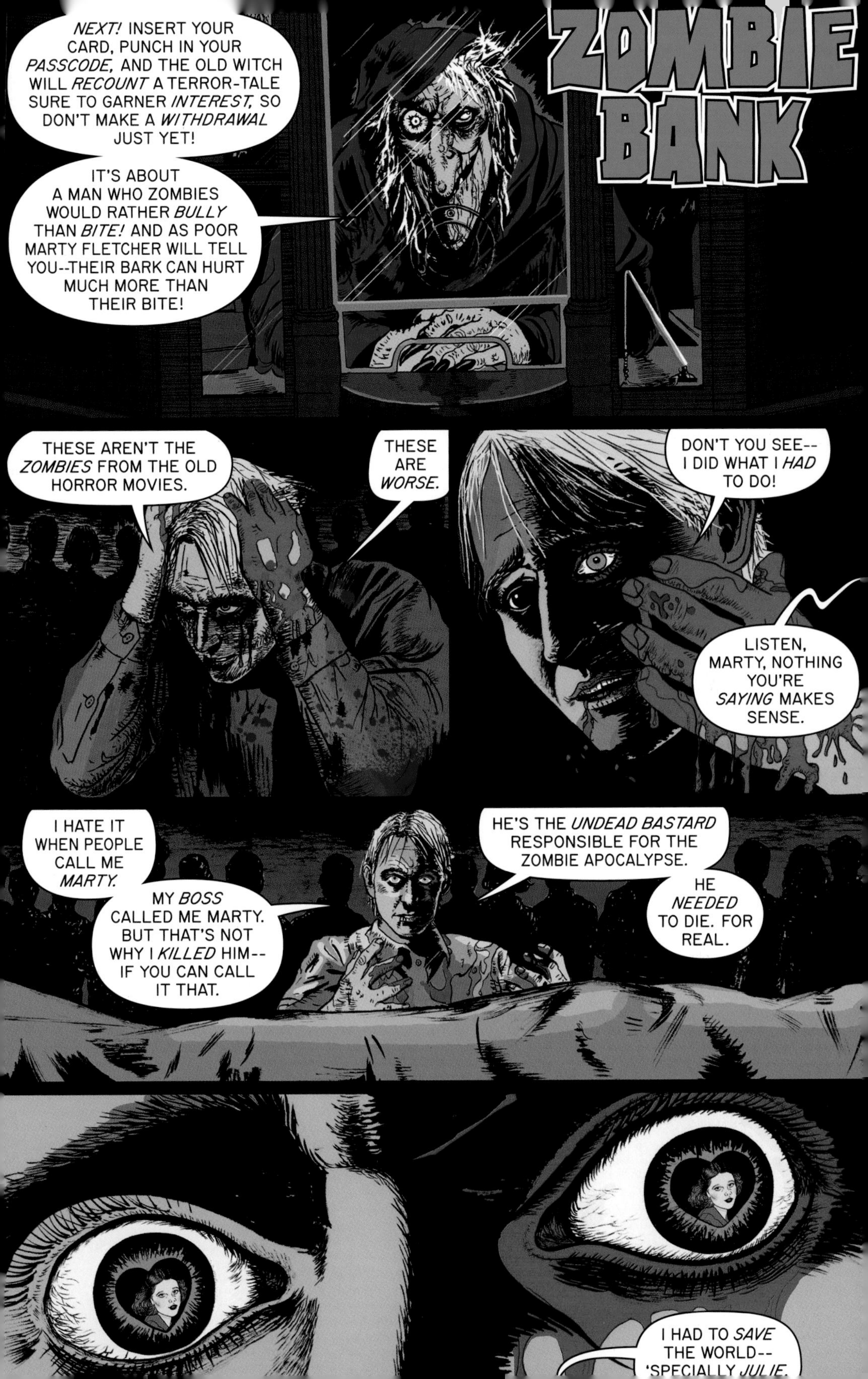
ZOMBIE BANK
NEXT! INSERT YOUR CARD, PUNCH IN YOUR PASSCODE, AND THE OLD WITCH WILL RECOUNT A TERROR-TALE SURE TO GARNER INTEREST, SO DON'T MAKE A WITHDRAWAL JUST YET!
IT'S ABOUT A MAN WHO ZOMBIES WOULD RATHER BULLY THAN BITE! AND AS POOR MARTY FLETCHER WILL TELL YOU--THEIR BARK CAN HURT MUCH MORE THAN THEIR BITE!
THESE AREN'T THE ZOMBIES FROM THE OLD HORROR MOVIES.
THESE ARE WORSE.
DON'T YOU SEE-- I DID WHAT I HAD TO DO!
LISTEN, MARTY, NOTHING YOU'RE SAYING MAKES SENSE.
I HATE IT WHEN PEOPLE CALL ME MARTY.
MY BOSS CALLED ME MARTY. BUT THAT'S NOT WHY I KILLED HIM-- IF YOU CAN CALL IT THAT.
HE'S THE UNDEAD BASTARD RESPONSIBLE FOR THE ZOMBIE APOCALYPSE.
HE NEEDED TO DIE. FOR REAL.
I HAD TO SAVE THE WORLD-- 'SPECIALLY JULIE.

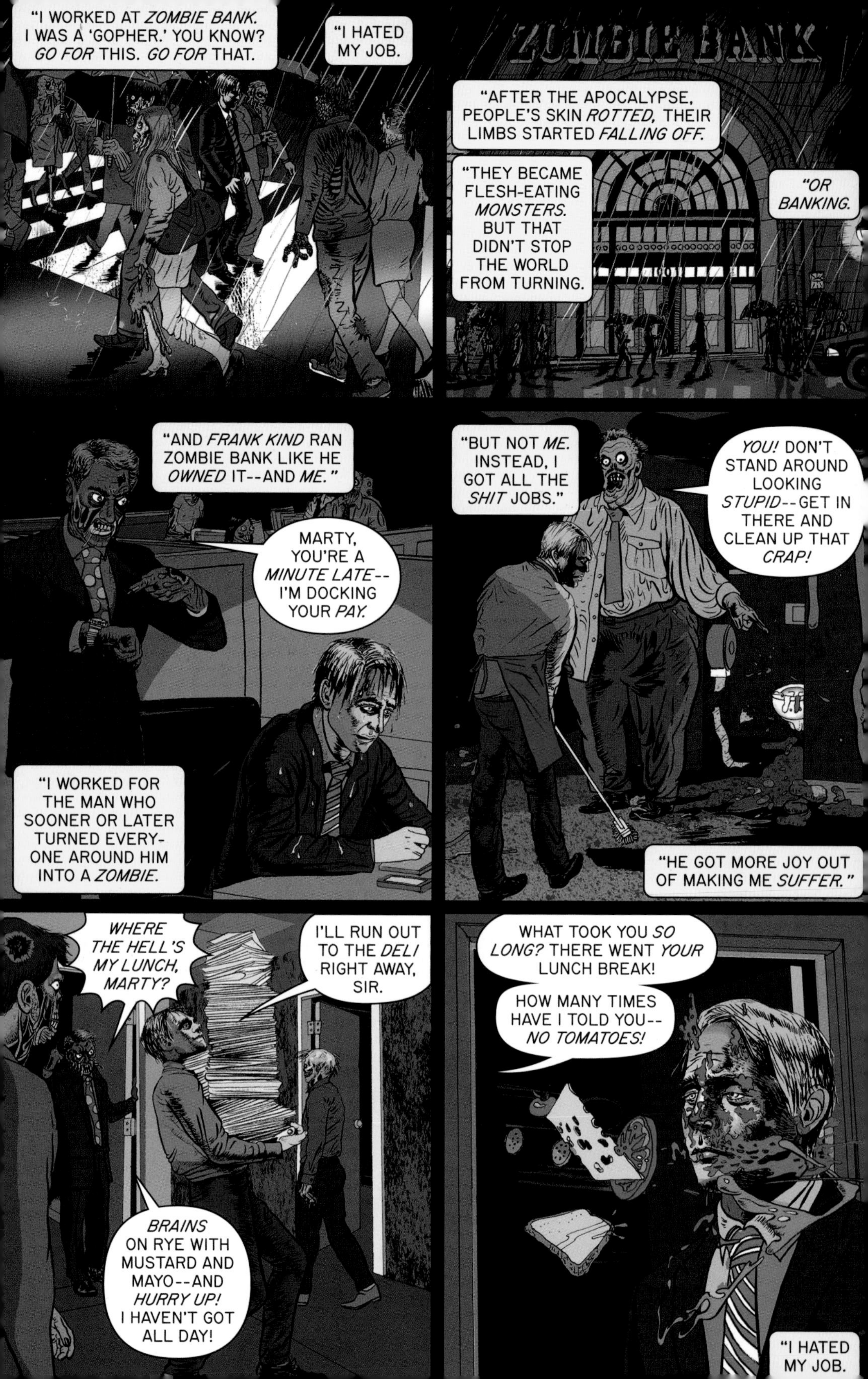
"I WORKED AT *ZOMBIE BANK.* I WAS A 'GOPHER.' YOU KNOW? *GO FOR* THIS. *GO FOR* THAT.
"I HATED MY JOB.
ZOMBIE BANK
"AFTER THE APOCALYPSE, PEOPLE'S SKIN *ROTTED,* THEIR LIMBS STARTED *FALLING OFF.*
"THEY BECAME FLESH-EATING *MONSTERS.* BUT THAT DIDN'T STOP THE WORLD FROM TURNING.
"OR BANKING.
"AND *FRANK KIND* RAN ZOMBIE BANK LIKE HE *OWNED* IT--AND *ME.*"
MARTY, YOU'RE A *MINUTE LATE*-- I'M DOCKING YOUR *PAY.*
"I WORKED FOR THE MAN WHO SOONER OR LATER TURNED EVERY-ONE AROUND HIM INTO A *ZOMBIE.*
"BUT NOT *ME.* INSTEAD, I GOT ALL THE *SHIT* JOBS."
YOU! DON'T STAND AROUND LOOKING *STUPID*--GET IN THERE AND CLEAN UP THAT *CRAP!*
"HE GOT MORE JOY OUT OF MAKING ME *SUFFER.*"
WHERE THE HELL'S MY LUNCH, MARTY?
I'LL RUN OUT TO THE *DELI* RIGHT AWAY, SIR.
BRAINS ON RYE WITH MUSTARD AND MAYO--AND *HURRY UP!* I HAVEN'T GOT ALL DAY!
WHAT TOOK YOU *SO LONG?* THERE WENT *YOUR* LUNCH BREAK!
HOW MANY TIMES HAVE I TOLD YOU-- *NO TOMATOES!*
"I HATED MY JOB.

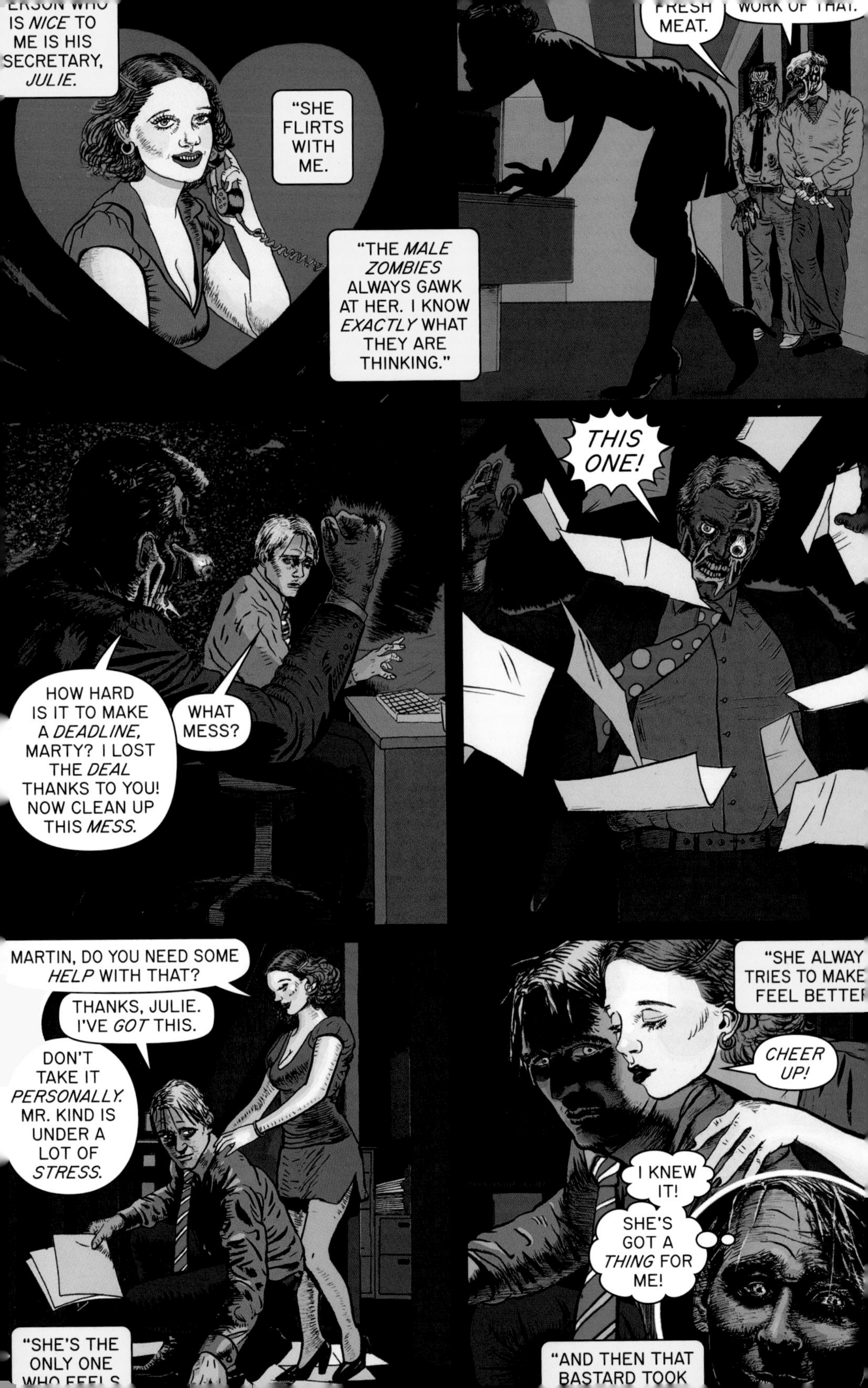
IS NICE TO ME IS HIS SECRETARY, JULIE.
"SHE FLIRTS WITH ME.
"THE MALE ZOMBIES ALWAYS GAWK AT HER. I KNOW EXACTLY WHAT THEY ARE THINKING."
MEAT.
HOW HARD IS IT TO MAKE A DEADLINE, MARTY? I LOST THE DEAL THANKS TO YOU! NOW CLEAN UP THIS MESS.
WHAT MESS?
THIS ONE!
MARTIN, DO YOU NEED SOME HELP WITH THAT?
THANKS, JULIE. I'VE GOT THIS.
DON'T TAKE IT PERSONALLY. MR. KIND IS UNDER A LOT OF STRESS.
"SHE'S THE ONLY ONE
CHEER UP!
I KNEW IT!
SHE'S GOT A THING FOR ME!
"AND THEN THAT BASTARD TOOK

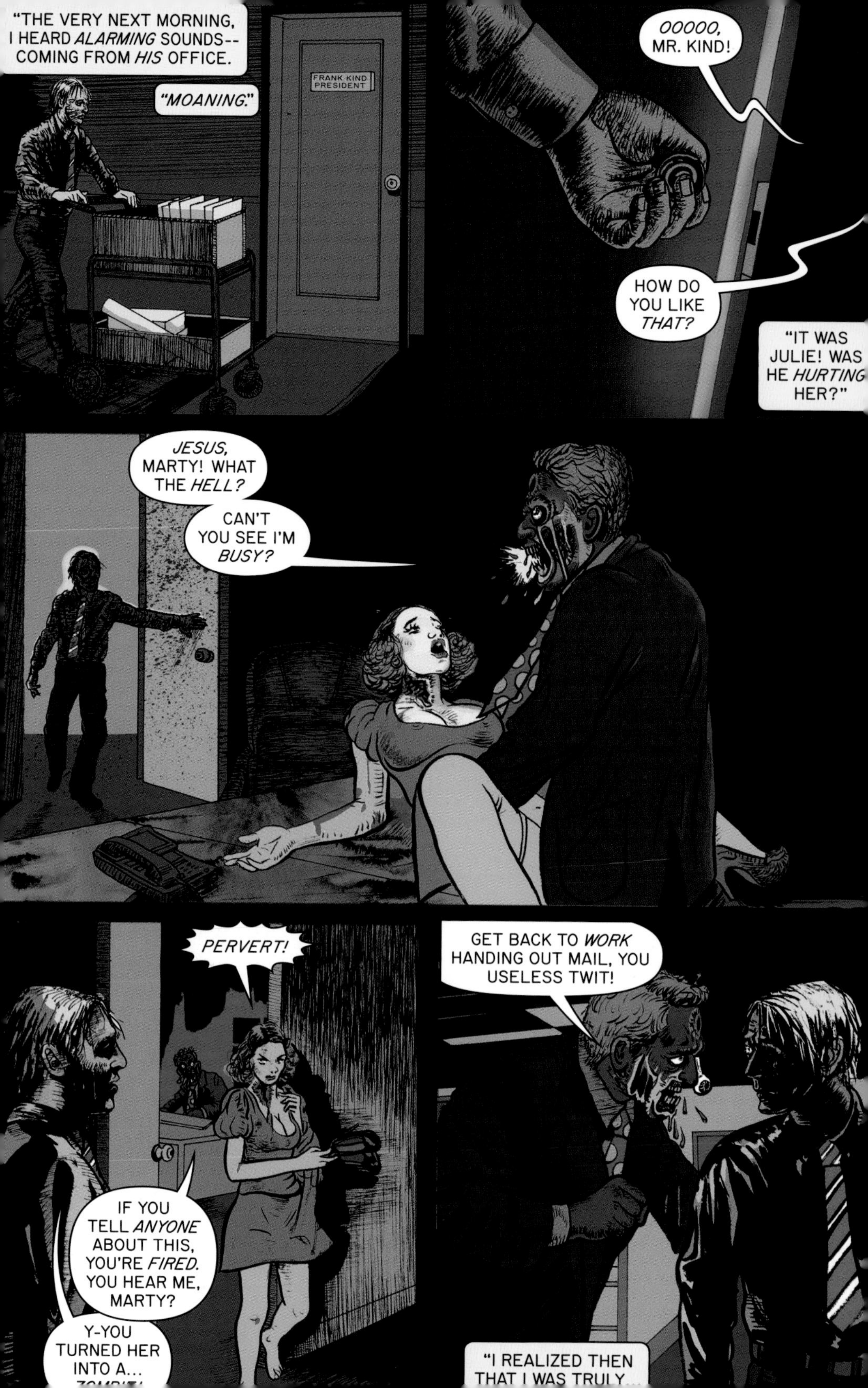
"THE VERY NEXT MORNING, I HEARD ALARMING SOUNDS-- COMING FROM HIS OFFICE.
"MOANING."
FRANK KIND PRESIDENT
OOOOO, MR. KIND!
HOW DO YOU LIKE THAT?
"IT WAS JULIE! WAS HE HURTING HER?"
JESUS, MARTY! WHAT THE HELL?
CAN'T YOU SEE I'M BUSY?
PERVERT!
GET BACK TO WORK HANDING OUT MAIL, YOU USELESS TWIT!
IF YOU TELL ANYONE ABOUT THIS, YOU'RE FIRED. YOU HEAR ME, MARTY?
Y-YOU TURNED HER INTO A...
"I REALIZED THEN THAT I WAS TRULY...

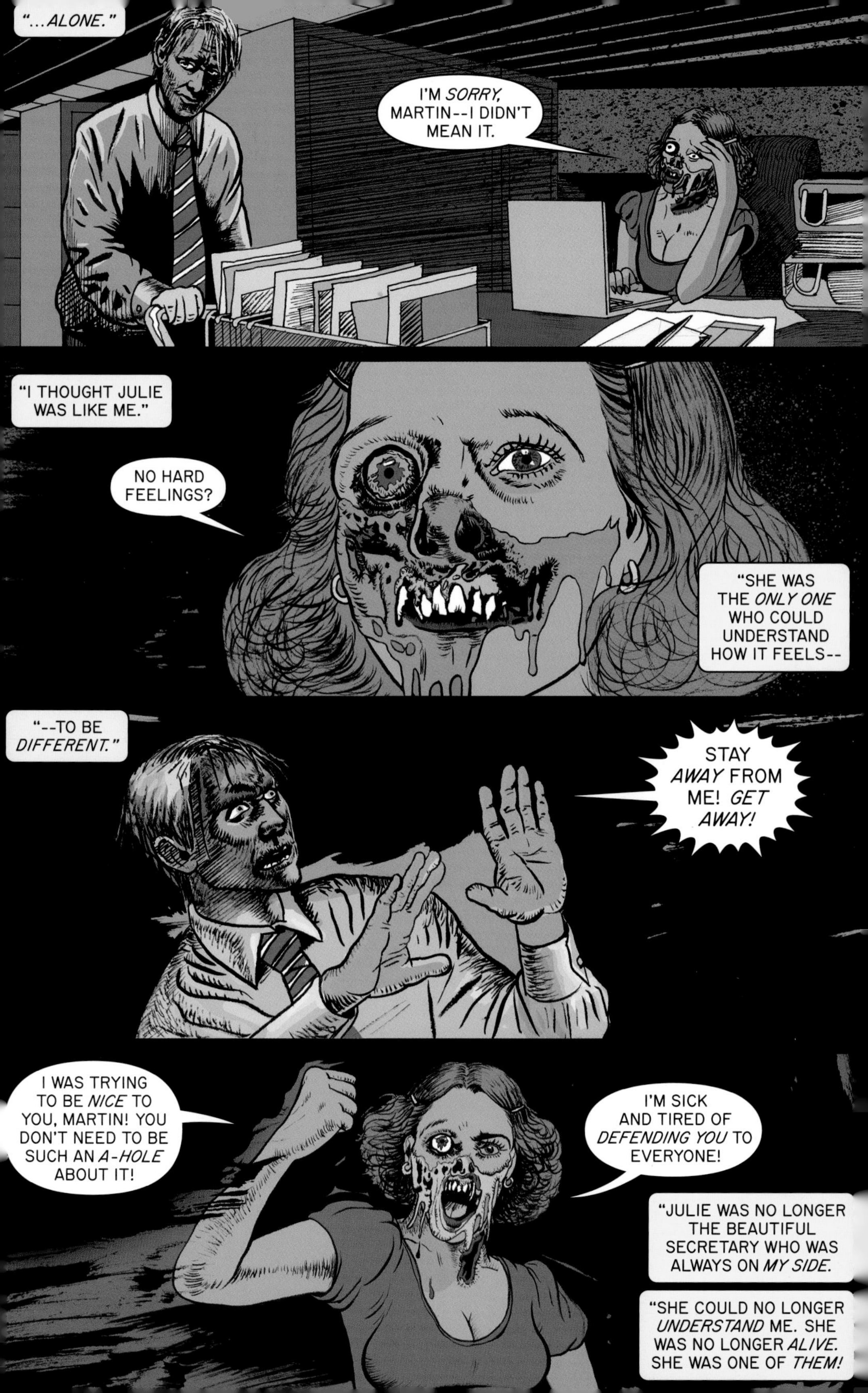
"...*ALONE.*"
I'M *SORRY,* MARTIN--I DIDN'T MEAN IT.
"I THOUGHT JULIE WAS LIKE ME."
NO HARD FEELINGS?
"SHE WAS THE *ONLY ONE* WHO COULD UNDERSTAND HOW IT FEELS--
"--TO BE *DIFFERENT.*"
STAY *AWAY* FROM ME! *GET AWAY!*
I WAS TRYING TO BE *NICE* TO YOU, MARTIN! YOU DON'T NEED TO BE SUCH AN *A-HOLE* ABOUT IT!
I'M SICK AND TIRED OF *DEFENDING YOU* TO EVERYONE!
"JULIE WAS NO LONGER THE BEAUTIFUL SECRETARY WHO WAS ALWAYS ON *MY SIDE.*
"SHE COULD NO LONGER *UNDERSTAND* ME. SHE WAS NO LONGER *ALIVE.* SHE WAS ONE OF *THEM!*

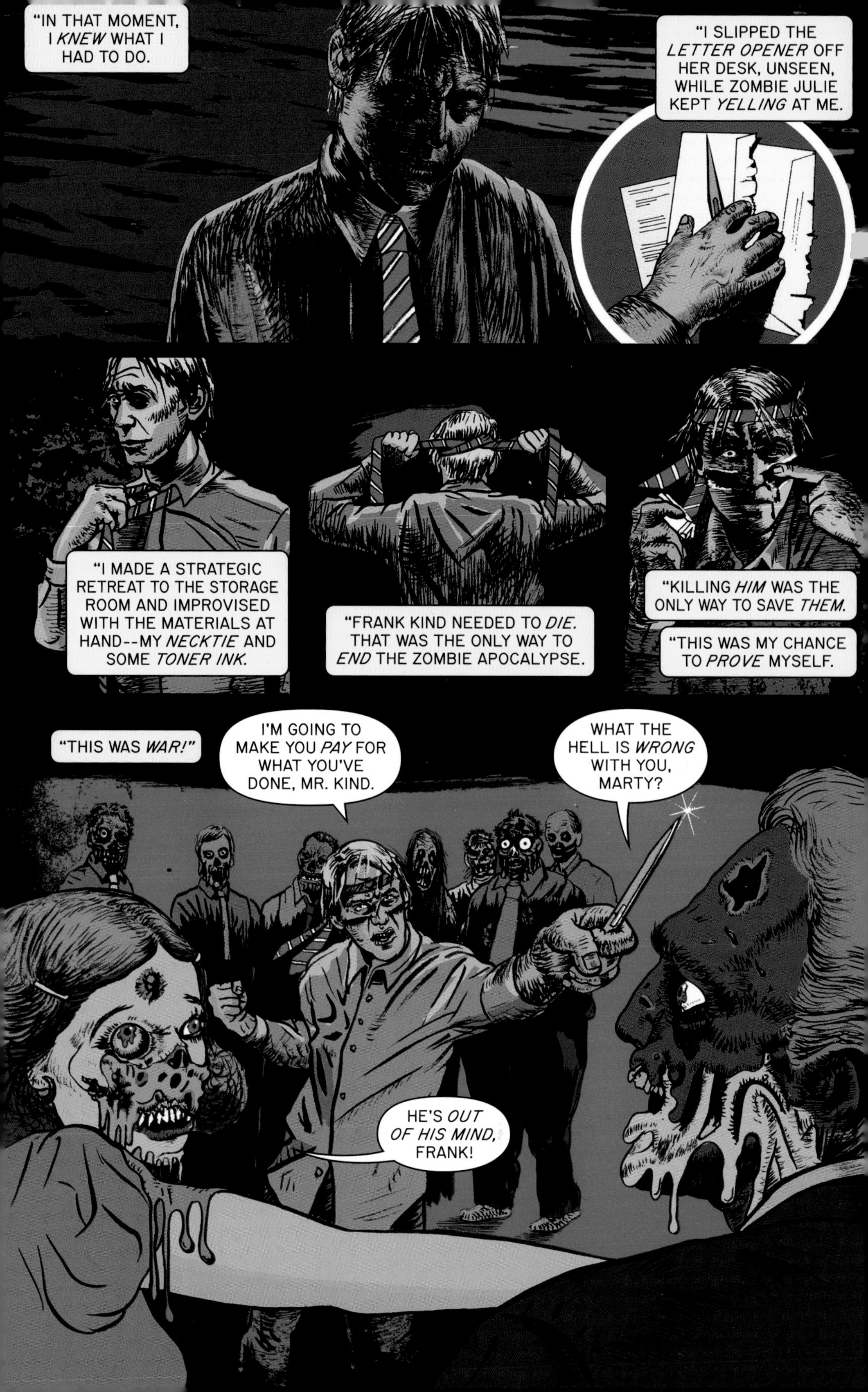
"IN THAT MOMENT, I *KNEW* WHAT I HAD TO DO.
"I SLIPPED THE *LETTER OPENER* OFF HER DESK, UNSEEN, WHILE ZOMBIE JULIE KEPT *YELLING* AT ME.
"I MADE A STRATEGIC RETREAT TO THE STORAGE ROOM AND IMPROVISED WITH THE MATERIALS AT HAND--MY *NECKTIE* AND SOME *TONER INK.*
"FRANK KIND NEEDED TO *DIE.* THAT WAS THE ONLY WAY TO *END* THE ZOMBIE APOCALYPSE.
"KILLING *HIM* WAS THE ONLY WAY TO SAVE *THEM.*
"THIS WAS MY CHANCE TO *PROVE* MYSELF.
"THIS WAS *WAR!*"
I'M GOING TO MAKE YOU *PAY* FOR WHAT YOU'VE DONE, MR. KIND.
WHAT THE HELL IS *WRONG* WITH YOU, MARTY?
HE'S *OUT OF HIS MIND,* FRANK!

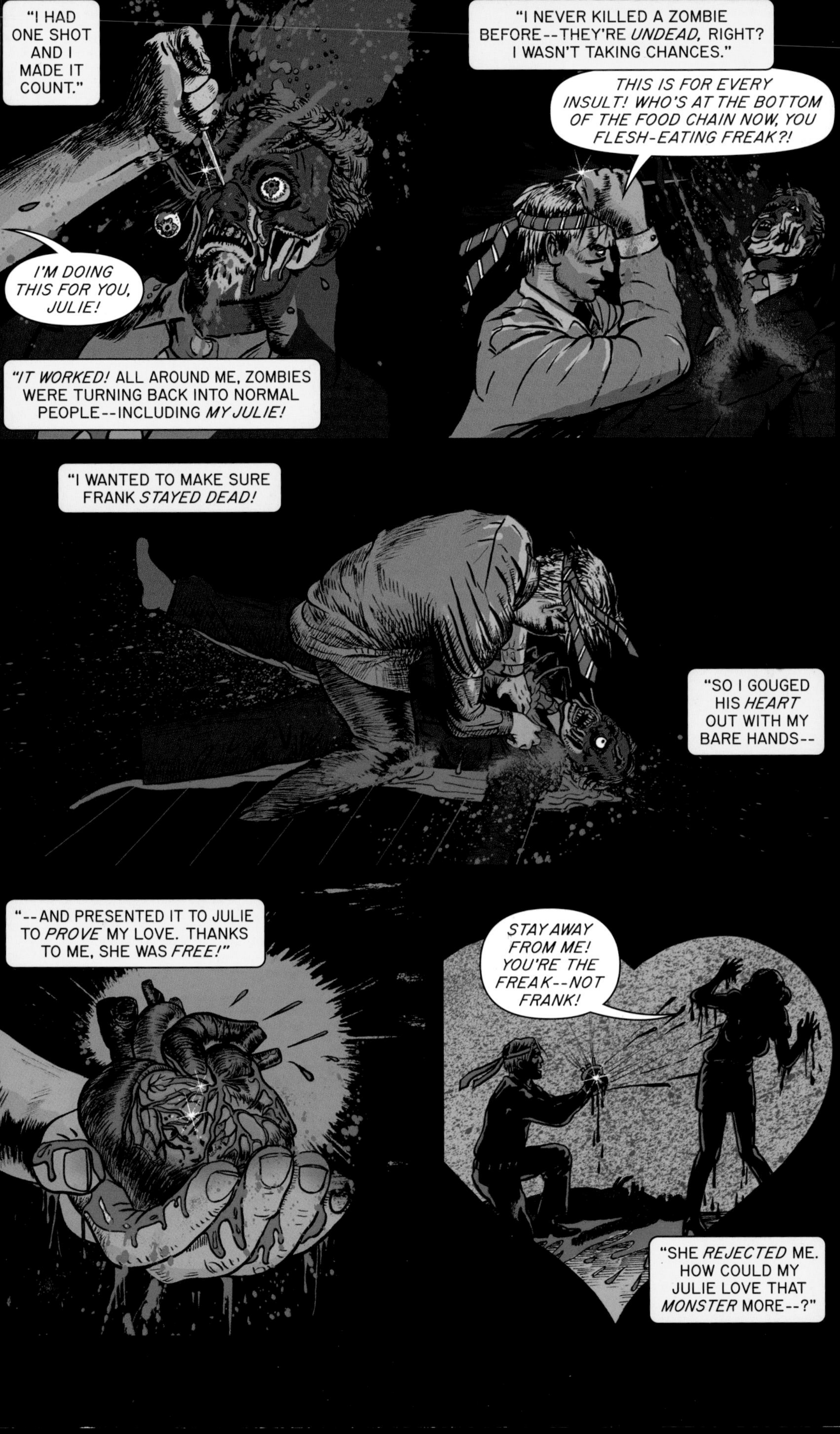
"I HAD ONE SHOT AND I MADE IT COUNT."
I'M DOING THIS FOR YOU, JULIE!
"IT WORKED! ALL AROUND ME, ZOMBIES WERE TURNING BACK INTO NORMAL PEOPLE--INCLUDING MY JULIE!
"I NEVER KILLED A ZOMBIE BEFORE--THEY'RE UNDEAD, RIGHT? I WASN'T TAKING CHANCES."
THIS IS FOR EVERY INSULT! WHO'S AT THE BOTTOM OF THE FOOD CHAIN NOW, YOU FLESH-EATING FREAK?!
"I WANTED TO MAKE SURE FRANK STAYED DEAD!
"SO I GOUGED HIS HEART OUT WITH MY BARE HANDS--
"--AND PRESENTED IT TO JULIE TO PROVE MY LOVE. THANKS TO ME, SHE WAS FREE!"
STAY AWAY FROM ME! YOU'RE THE FREAK--NOT FRANK!
"SHE REJECTED ME. HOW COULD MY JULIE LOVE THAT MONSTER MORE--?"

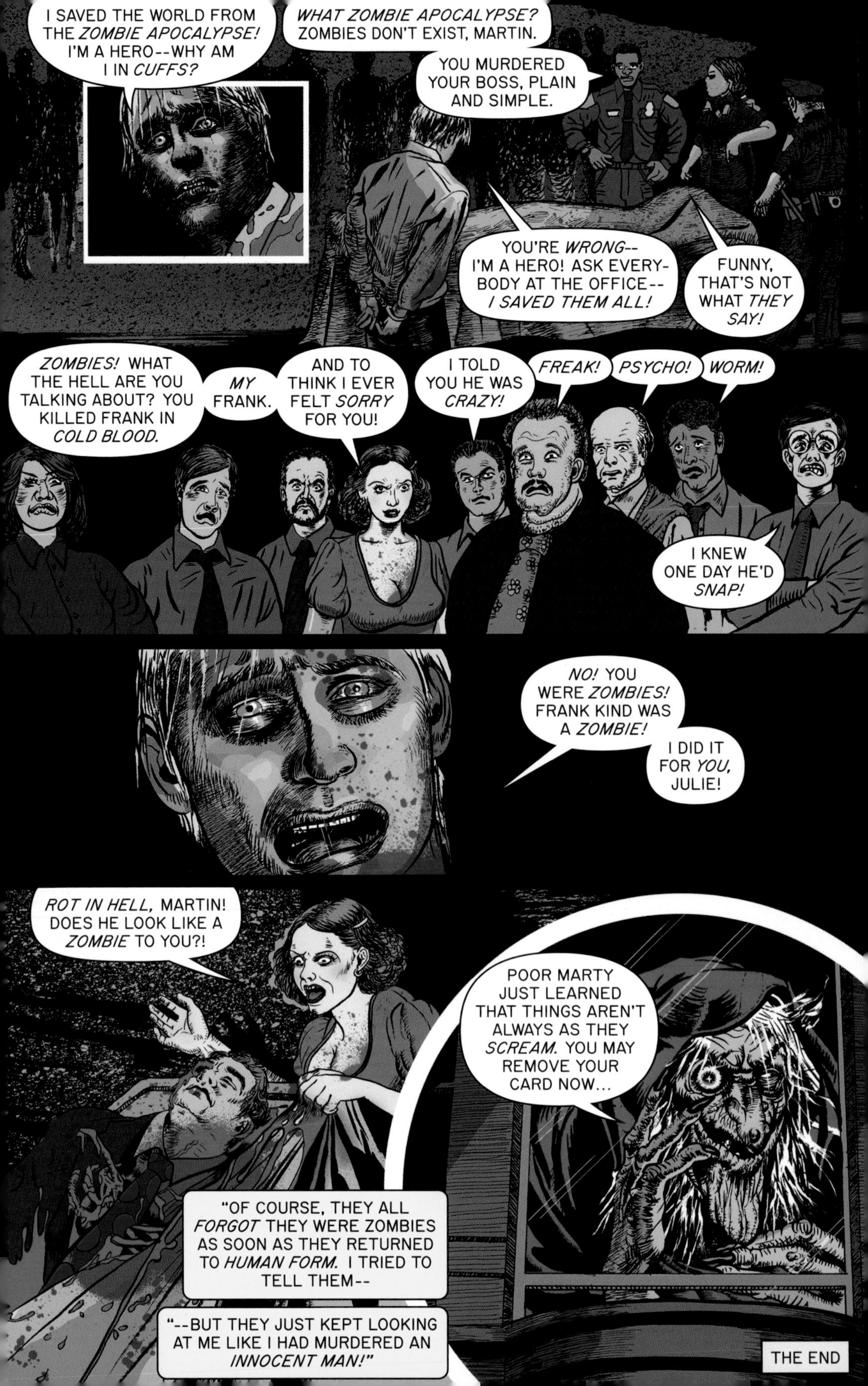

I SAVED THE WORLD FROM THE *ZOMBIE APOCALYPSE!* I'M A HERO--WHY AM I IN *CUFFS?*
WHAT ZOMBIE APOCALYPSE? ZOMBIES DON'T EXIST, MARTIN.
YOU MURDERED YOUR BOSS, PLAIN AND SIMPLE.
YOU'RE *WRONG*-- I'M A HERO! ASK EVERY-BODY AT THE OFFICE-- *I SAVED THEM ALL!*
FUNNY, THAT'S NOT WHAT *THEY SAY!*
ZOMBIES! WHAT THE HELL ARE YOU TALKING ABOUT? YOU KILLED FRANK IN *COLD BLOOD.*
MY FRANK.
AND TO THINK I EVER FELT *SORRY* FOR YOU!
I TOLD YOU HE WAS *CRAZY!*
FREAK!
PSYCHO!
WORM!
I KNEW ONE DAY HE'D *SNAP!*
NO! YOU WERE *ZOMBIES!* FRANK KIND WAS A *ZOMBIE!*
I DID IT FOR *YOU,* JULIE!
ROT IN HELL, MARTIN! DOES HE LOOK LIKE A *ZOMBIE* TO YOU?!
POOR MARTY JUST LEARNED THAT THINGS AREN'T ALWAYS AS THEY *SCREAM.* YOU MAY REMOVE YOUR CARD NOW...
"OF COURSE, THEY ALL *FORGOT* THEY WERE ZOMBIES AS SOON AS THEY RETURNED TO *HUMAN FORM.* I TRIED TO TELL THEM--
"--BUT THEY JUST KEPT LOOKING AT ME LIKE I HAD MURDERED AN *INNOCENT MAN!*"
THE END

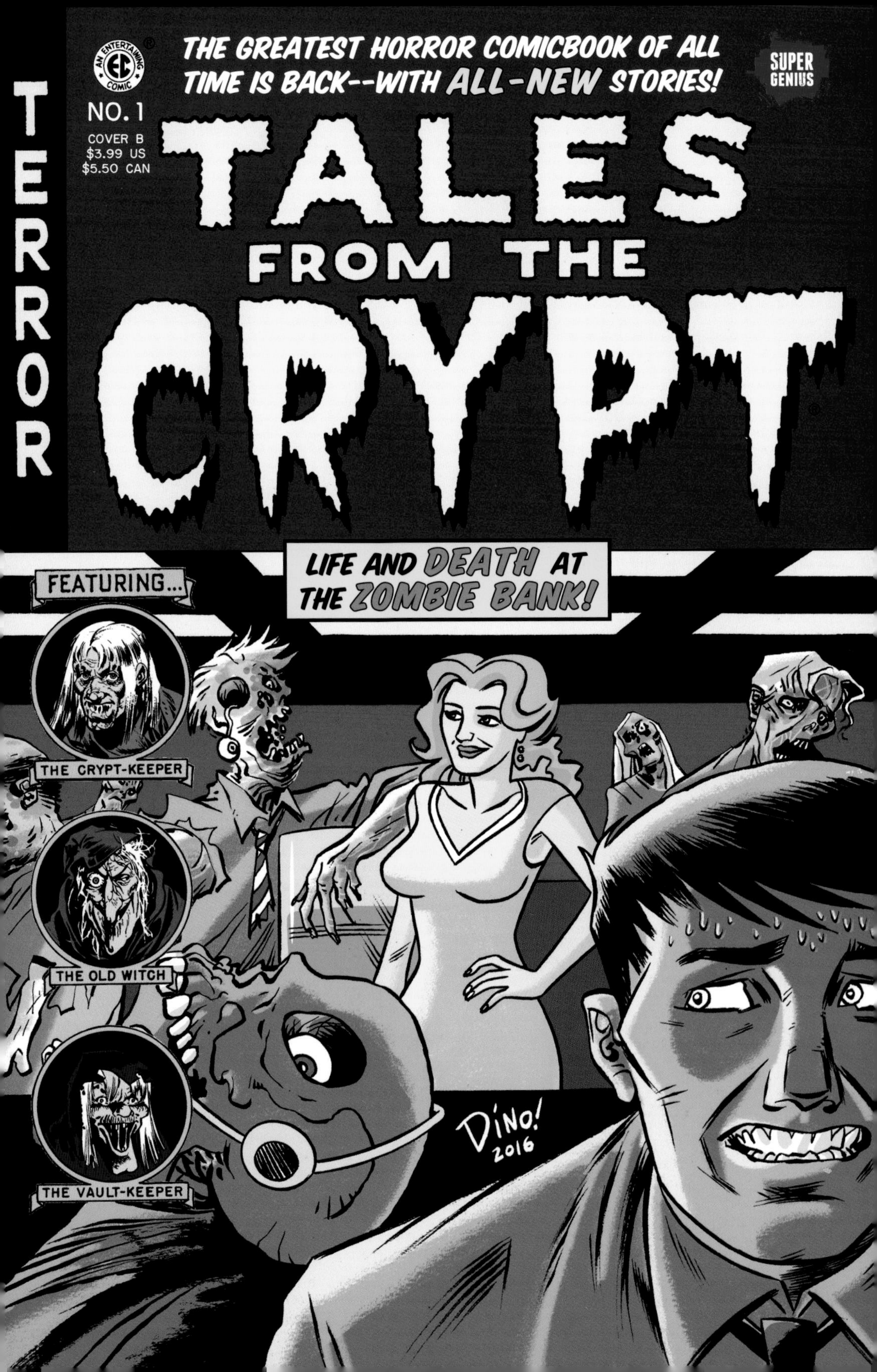

THE GREATEST HORROR COMICBOOK OF ALL TIME IS BACK--WITH ALL-NEW STORIES!
AN ENTERTAINING EC COMIC
SUPER GENIUS
NO. 1
COVER B
$3.99 US
$5.50 CAN
TERROR
TALES FROM THE CRYPT
LIFE AND DEATH AT THE ZOMBIE BANK!
FEATURING...
THE CRYPT-KEEPER
THE OLD WITCH
THE VAULT-KEEPER
DINO! 2016

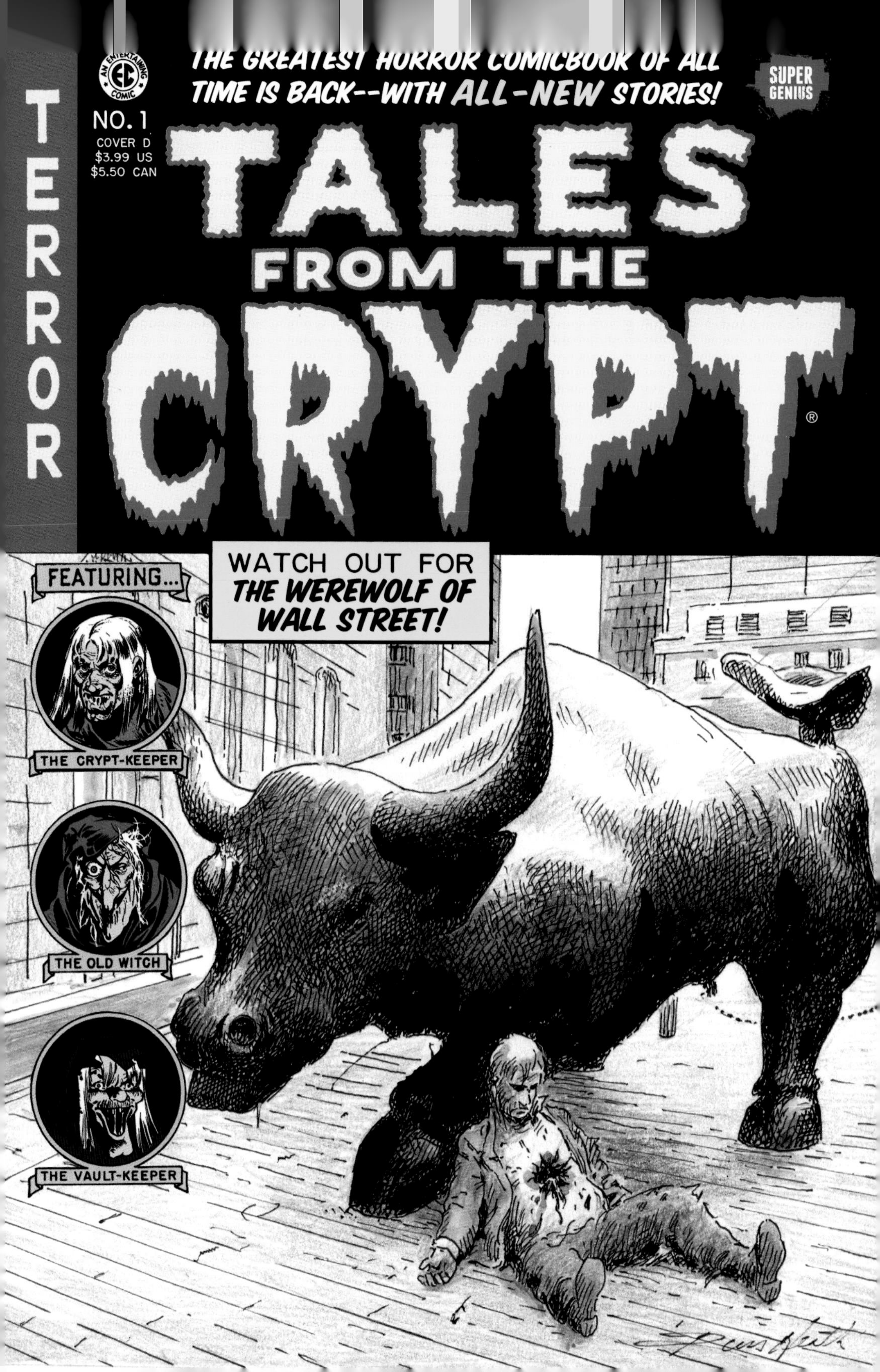
THE GREATEST HORROR COMICBOOK OF ALL TIME IS BACK--WITH ALL-NEW STORIES!
AN ENTERTAINING COMIC
SUPER GENIUS
NO. 1
COVER D
$3.99 US
$5.50 CAN
TERROR
TALES FROM THE CRYPT®
WATCH OUT FOR THE WEREWOLF OF WALL STREET!
FEATURING...
THE CRYPT-KEEPER
THE OLD WITCH
THE VAULT-KEEPER

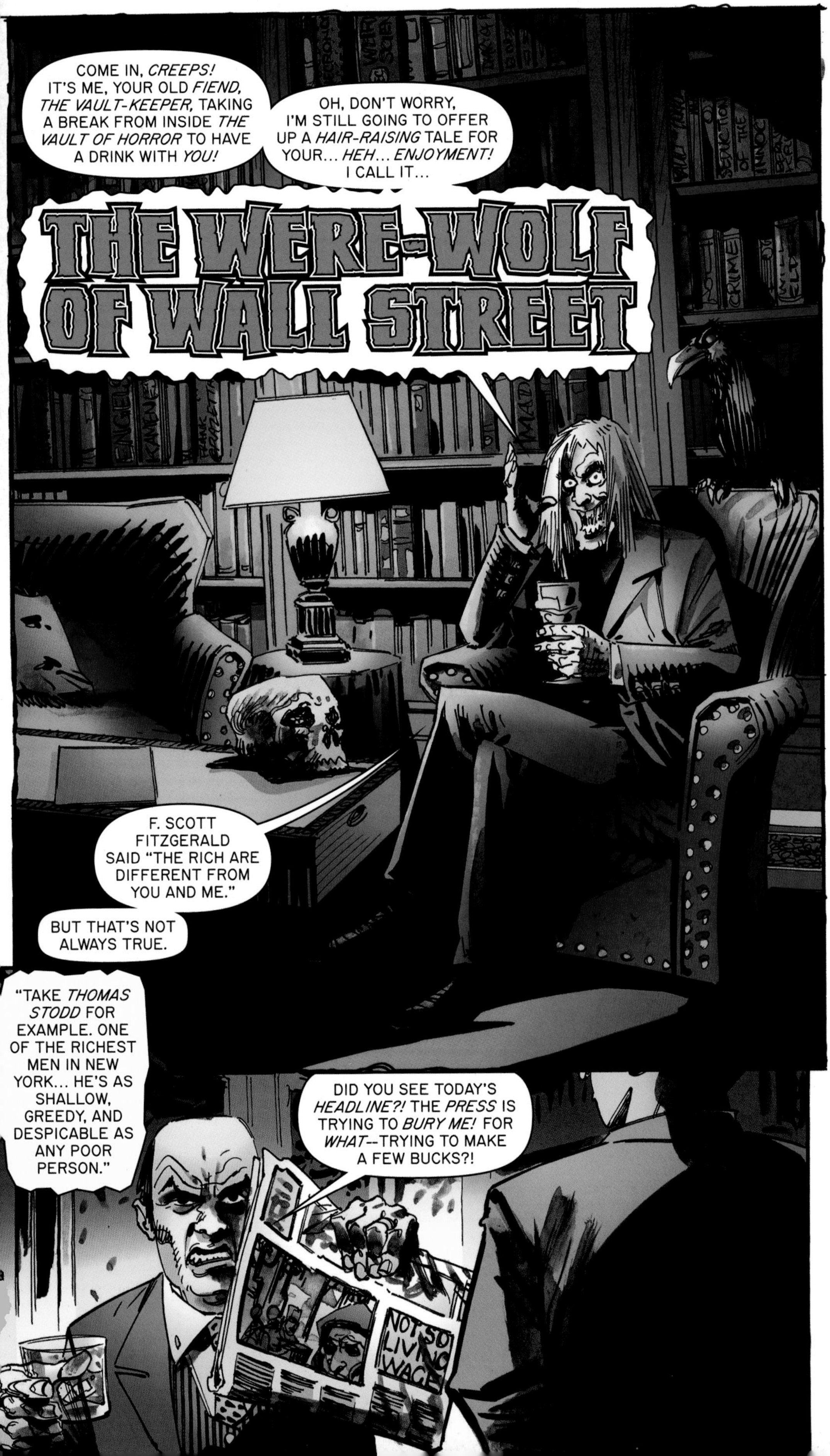

COME IN, *CREEPS!* IT'S ME, YOUR OLD *FIEND, THE VAULT-KEEPER,* TAKING A BREAK FROM INSIDE *THE VAULT OF HORROR* TO HAVE A DRINK WITH *YOU!*
OH, DON'T WORRY, I'M STILL GOING TO OFFER UP A *HAIR-RAISING* TALE FOR YOUR... *HEH... ENJOYMENT!* I CALL IT...
THE WERE-WOLF OF WALL STREET
F. SCOTT FITZGERALD SAID "THE RICH ARE DIFFERENT FROM YOU AND ME."
BUT THAT'S NOT ALWAYS TRUE.
"TAKE *THOMAS STODD* FOR EXAMPLE. ONE OF THE RICHEST MEN IN NEW YORK... HE'S AS SHALLOW, GREEDY, AND DESPICABLE AS ANY POOR PERSON."
DID YOU SEE TODAY'S *HEADLINE?!* THE *PRESS* IS TRYING TO *BURY ME!* FOR *WHAT*--TRYING TO MAKE A FEW BUCKS?!

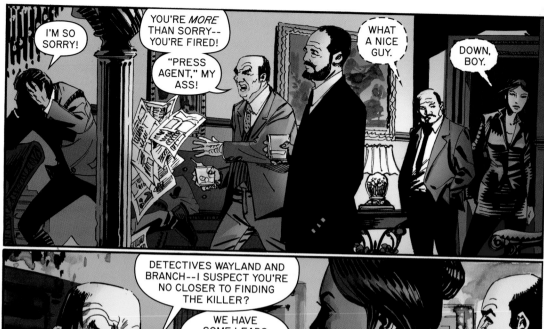

I'M SO SORRY!

YOU'RE *MORE* THAN SORRY-- YOU'RE FIRED!

"PRESS AGENT," MY ASS!

WHAT A NICE GUY.

DOWN, BOY.

DETECTIVES WAYLAND AND BRANCH--I SUSPECT YOU'RE NO CLOSER TO FINDING THE KILLER?

WE HAVE SOME LEADS WE'RE FOLLOWING, MR. STODD.

THERE IS NO SHORTAGE OF SUSPECTS IN THE MURDERS OF YOUR OTHER THREE PARTNERS.

IT WOULD BE MORE FRUITFUL IF YOU WOULD COOPERATE WITH OUR INVESTIGATION.

OF COURSE WE UNDERSTAND THE IMPORTANCE OF RESPECTING YOUR RIGHT TO PRIVACY, BUT--

--BUT YOU ARE NOT ABOVE WASTING MY TIME, OBVIOUSLY. THANK YOU ANYWAY, BUT I'LL PUT MY TRUST IN MY OWN PRIVATE SECURITY FIRM.

GOOD NIGHT, DETECTIVES.

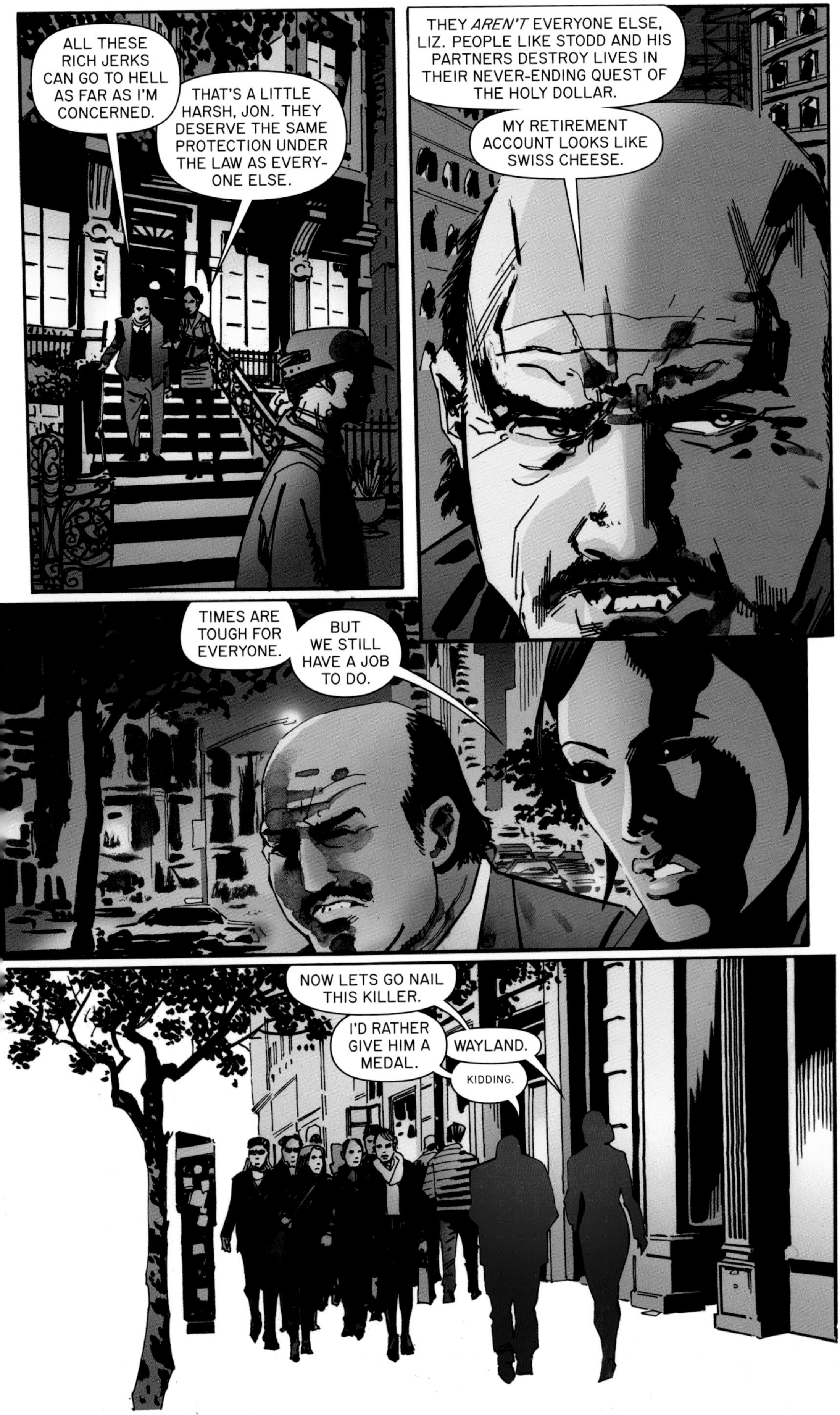
ALL THESE RICH JERKS CAN GO TO HELL AS FAR AS I'M CONCERNED.
THAT'S A LITTLE HARSH, JON. THEY DESERVE THE SAME PROTECTION UNDER THE LAW AS EVERY-ONE ELSE.
THEY *AREN'T* EVERYONE ELSE, LIZ. PEOPLE LIKE STODD AND HIS PARTNERS DESTROY LIVES IN THEIR NEVER-ENDING QUEST OF THE HOLY DOLLAR.
MY RETIREMENT ACCOUNT LOOKS LIKE SWISS CHEESE.
TIMES ARE TOUGH FOR EVERYONE.
BUT WE STILL HAVE A JOB TO DO.
NOW LETS GO NAIL THIS KILLER.
I'D RATHER GIVE HIM A MEDAL.
WAYLAND.
KIDDING.

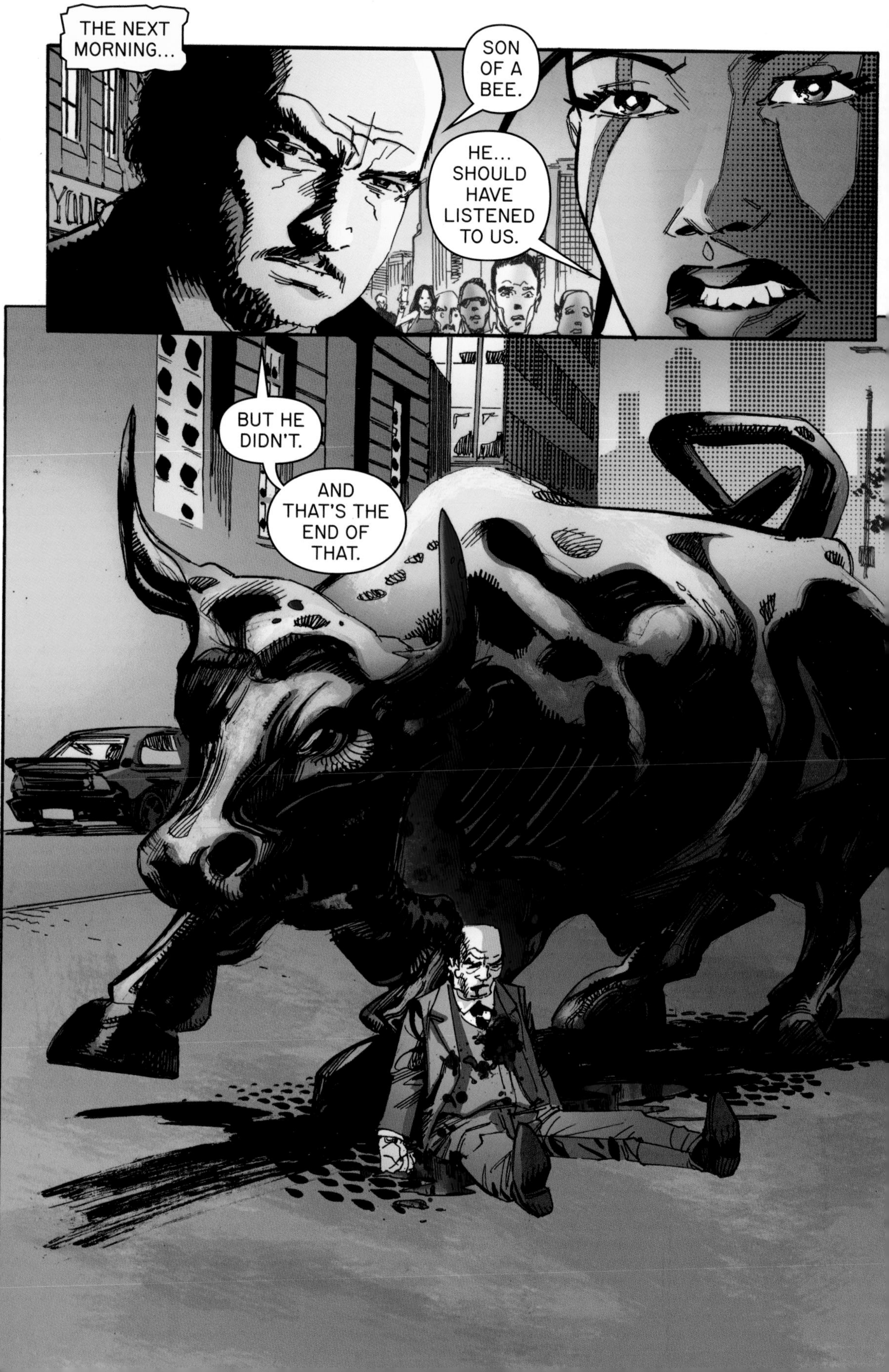
THE NEXT MORNING...
SON OF A BEE.
HE... SHOULD HAVE LISTENED TO US.
BUT HE DIDN'T.
AND THAT'S THE END OF THAT.

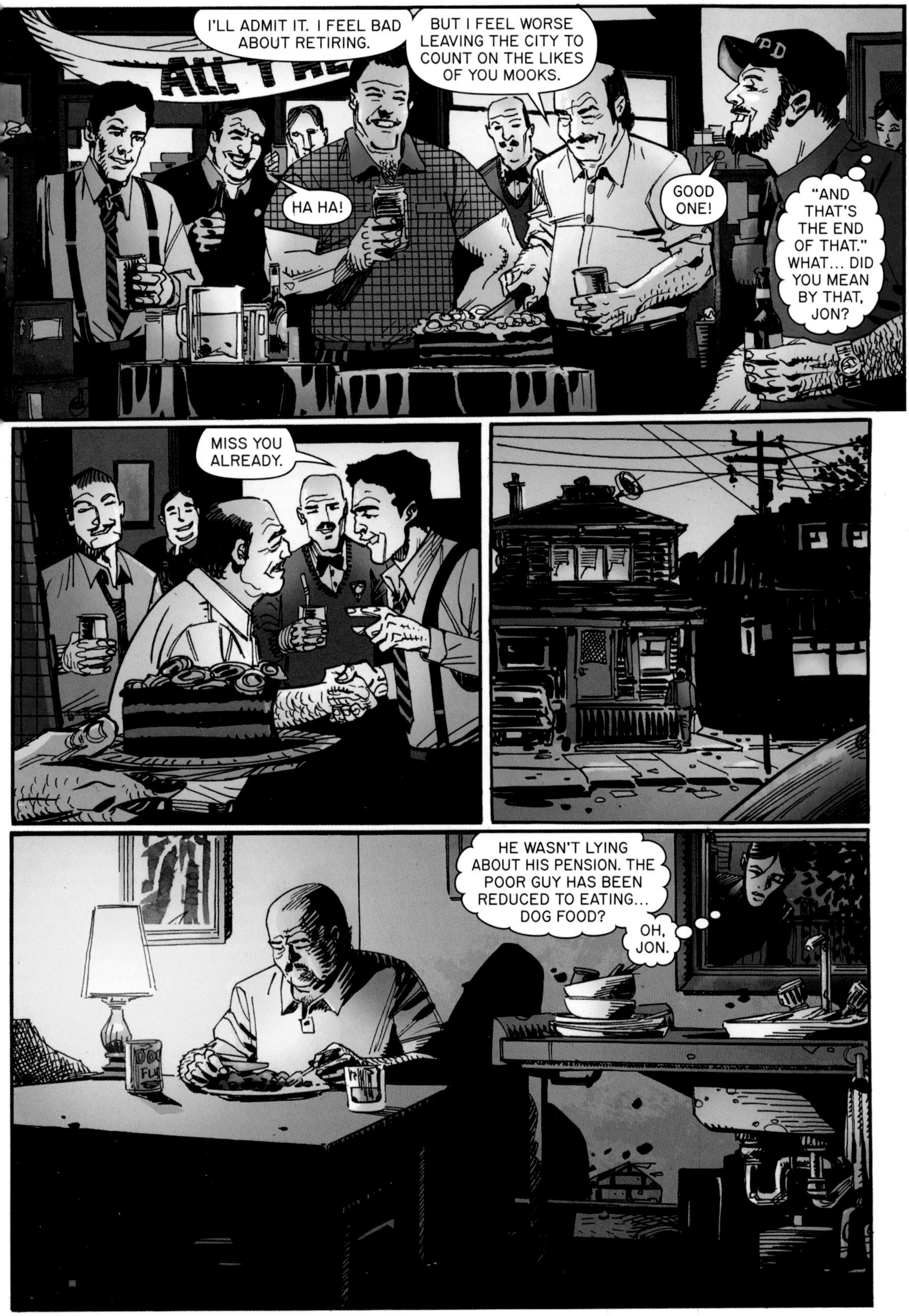
I'LL ADMIT IT. I FEEL BAD ABOUT RETIRING.
BUT I FEEL WORSE LEAVING THE CITY TO COUNT ON THE LIKES OF YOU MOOKS.
HA HA!
GOOD ONE!
"AND THAT'S THE END OF THAT." WHAT... DID YOU MEAN BY THAT, JON?
MISS YOU ALREADY.
HE WASN'T LYING ABOUT HIS PENSION. THE POOR GUY HAS BEEN REDUCED TO EATING... DOG FOOD?
OH, JON.

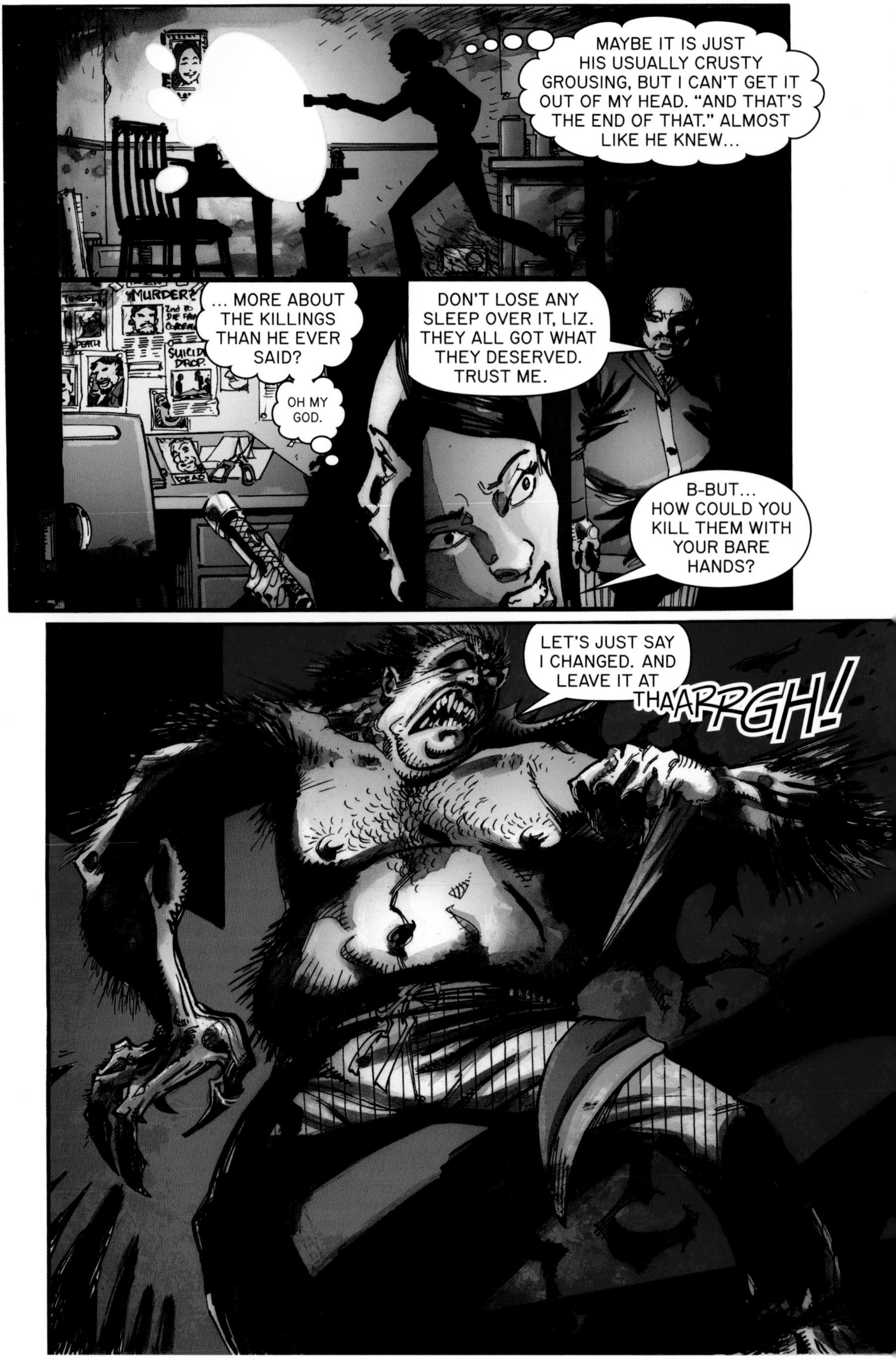
MAYBE IT IS JUST HIS USUALLY CRUSTY GROUSING, BUT I CAN'T GET IT OUT OF MY HEAD. "AND THAT'S THE END OF THAT." ALMOST LIKE HE KNEW...
... MORE ABOUT THE KILLINGS THAN HE EVER SAID?
OH MY GOD.
DON'T LOSE ANY SLEEP OVER IT, LIZ. THEY ALL GOT WHAT THEY DESERVED. TRUST ME.
B-BUT... HOW COULD YOU KILL THEM WITH YOUR BARE HANDS?
LET'S JUST SAY I CHANGED. AND LEAVE IT AT
THAARRGH!

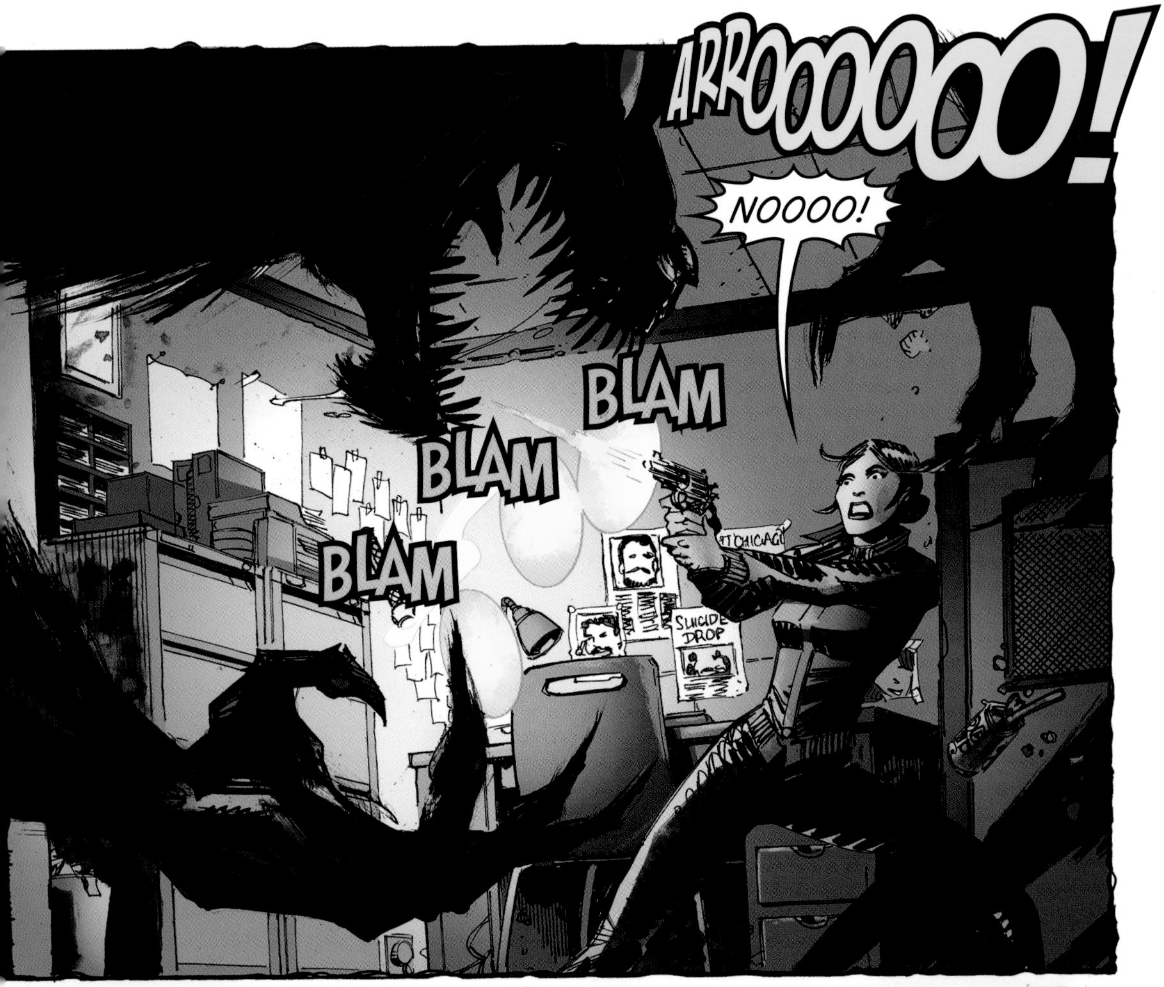
ARROOOOOO!
NOOOO!
BLAM
BLAM
BLAM
CHICAGO
SUICIDE DROP

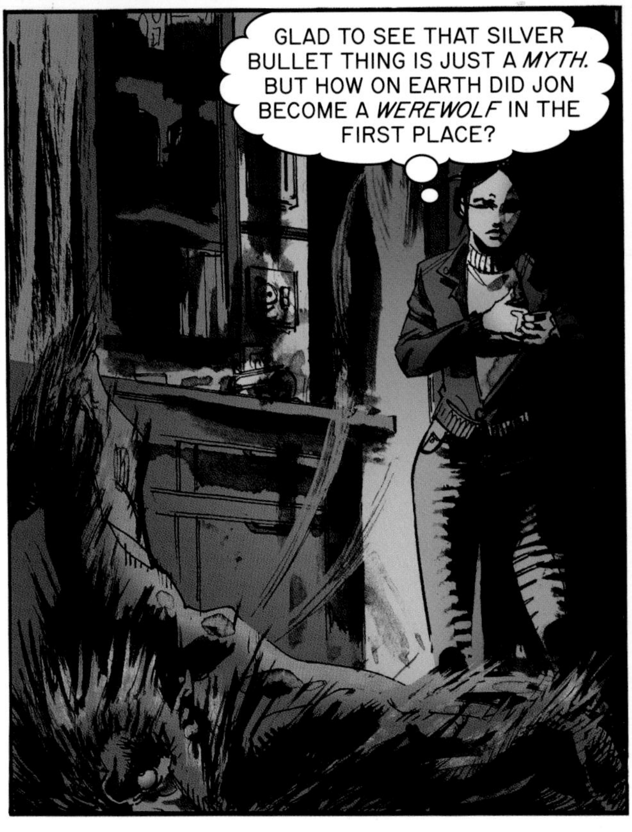
GLAD TO SEE THAT SILVER BULLET THING IS JUST A *MYTH.* BUT HOW ON EARTH DID JON BECOME A *WEREWOLF* IN THE FIRST PLACE?

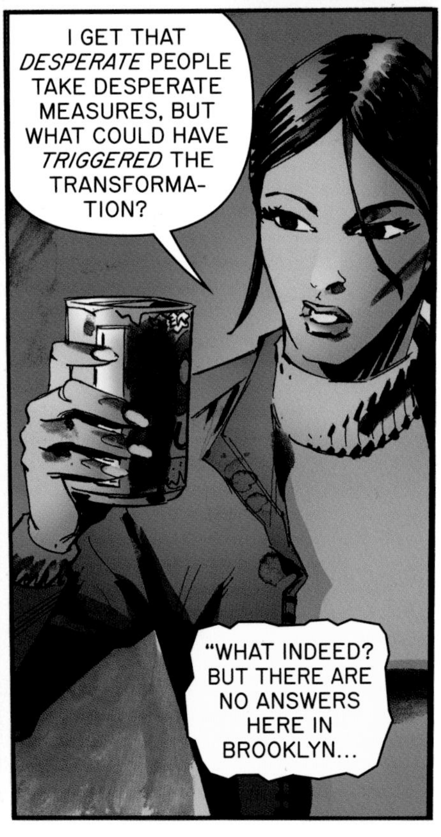
I GET THAT *DESPERATE* PEOPLE TAKE DESPERATE MEASURES, BUT WHAT COULD HAVE *TRIGGERED* THE TRANSFORMA-TION?
"WHAT INDEED? BUT THERE ARE NO ANSWERS HERE IN BROOKLYN...

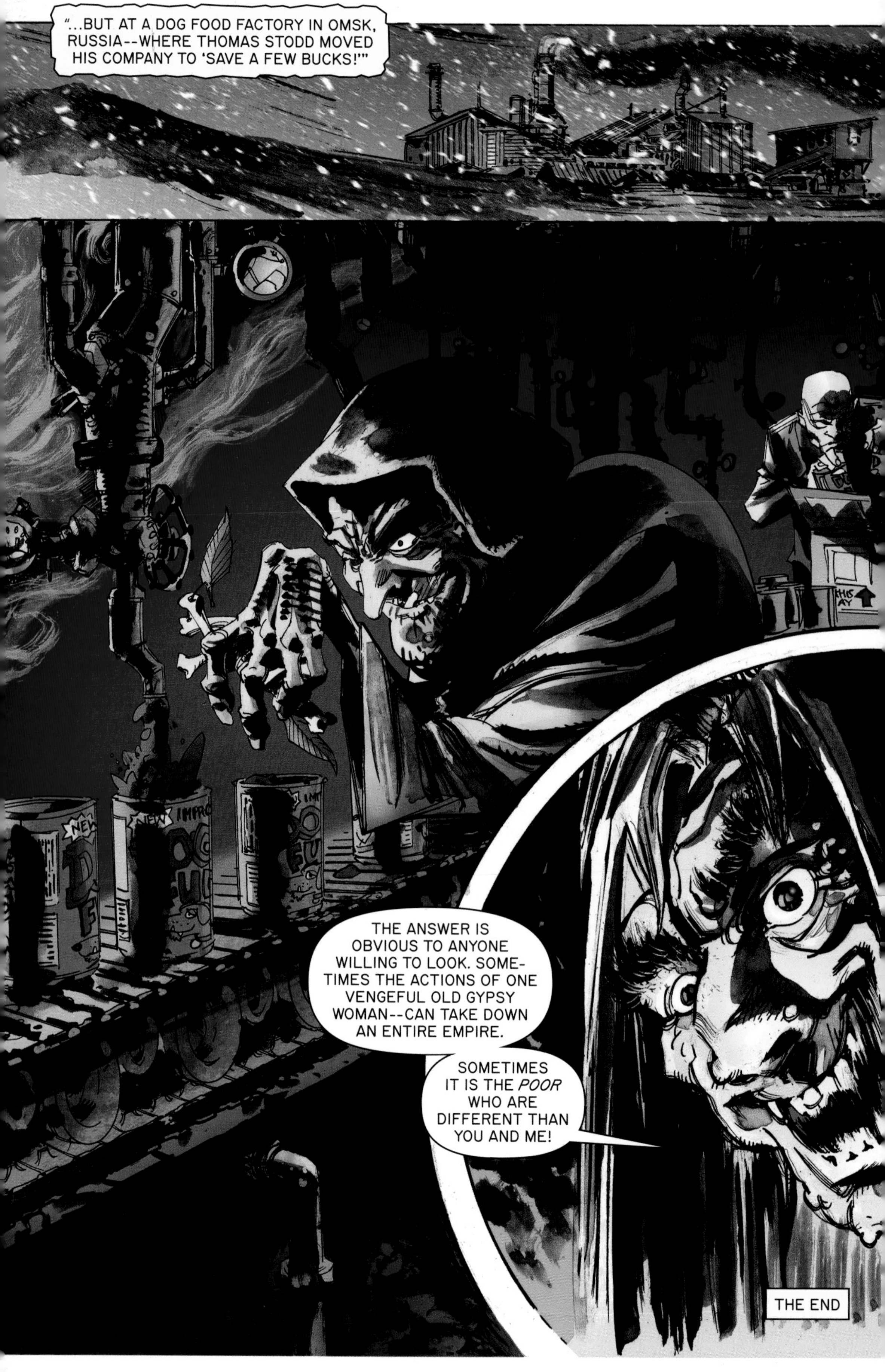
"...BUT AT A DOG FOOD FACTORY IN OMSK, RUSSIA--WHERE THOMAS STODD MOVED HIS COMPANY TO 'SAVE A FEW BUCKS!'"
THE ANSWER IS OBVIOUS TO ANYONE WILLING TO LOOK. SOMETIMES THE ACTIONS OF ONE VENGEFUL OLD GYPSY WOMAN--CAN TAKE DOWN AN ENTIRE EMPIRE.
SOMETIMES IT IS THE *POOR* WHO ARE DIFFERENT THAN YOU AND ME!
THE END

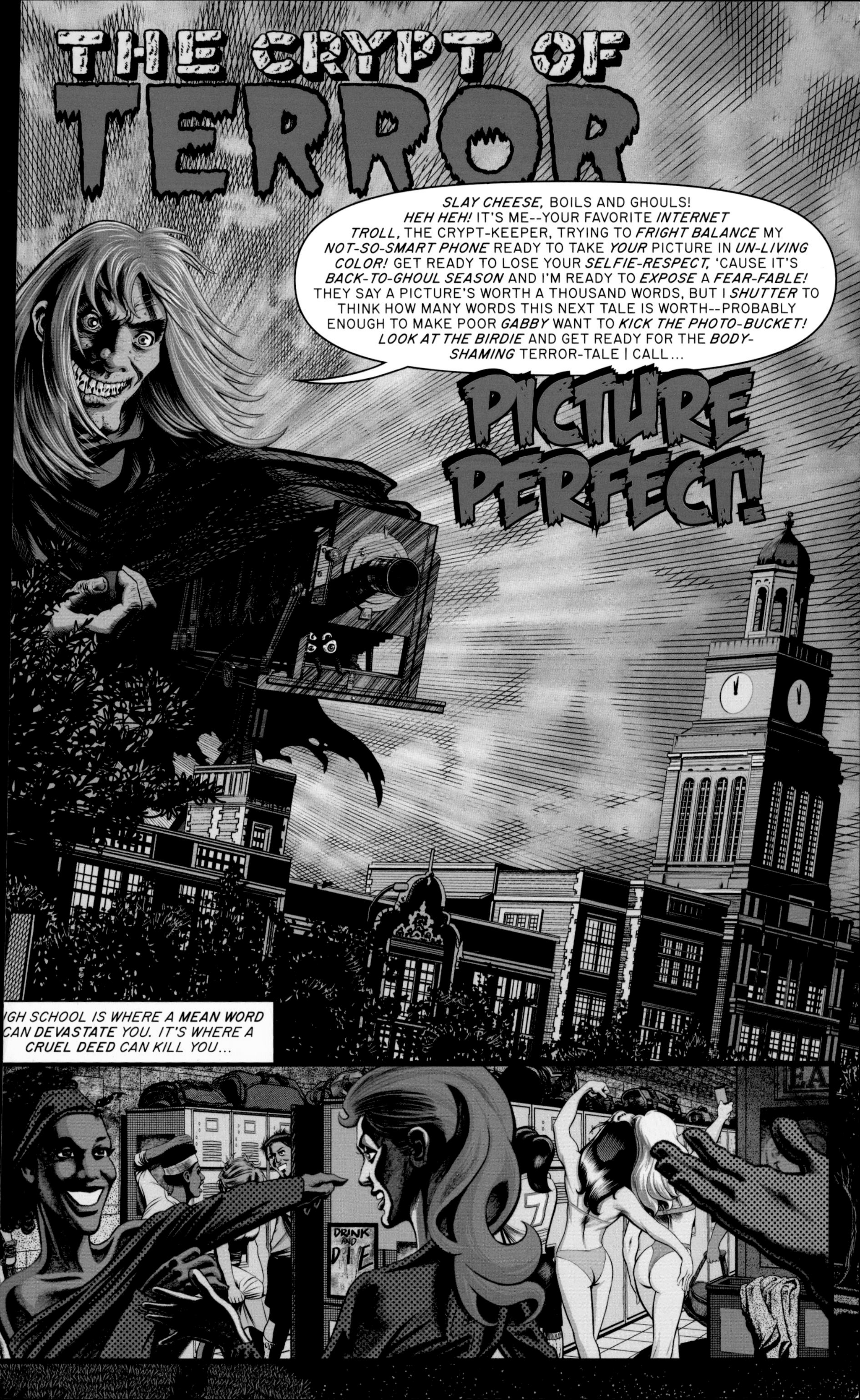
THE CRYPT OF TERROR
SLAY CHEESE, BOILS AND GHOULS! HEH HEH! IT'S ME--YOUR FAVORITE INTERNET TROLL, THE CRYPT-KEEPER, TRYING TO FRIGHT BALANCE MY NOT-SO-SMART PHONE READY TO TAKE YOUR PICTURE IN UN-LIVING COLOR! GET READY TO LOSE YOUR SELFIE-RESPECT, 'CAUSE IT'S BACK-TO-GHOUL SEASON AND I'M READY TO EXPOSE A FEAR-FABLE! THEY SAY A PICTURE'S WORTH A THOUSAND WORDS, BUT I SHUTTER TO THINK HOW MANY WORDS THIS NEXT TALE IS WORTH--PROBABLY ENOUGH TO MAKE POOR GABBY WANT TO KICK THE PHOTO-BUCKET! LOOK AT THE BIRDIE AND GET READY FOR THE BODY-SHAMING TERROR-TALE I CALL...
PICTURE PERFECT!
IGH SCHOOL IS WHERE A MEAN WORD CAN DEVASTATE YOU. IT'S WHERE A CRUEL DEED CAN KILL YOU...
DRINK AND DIE

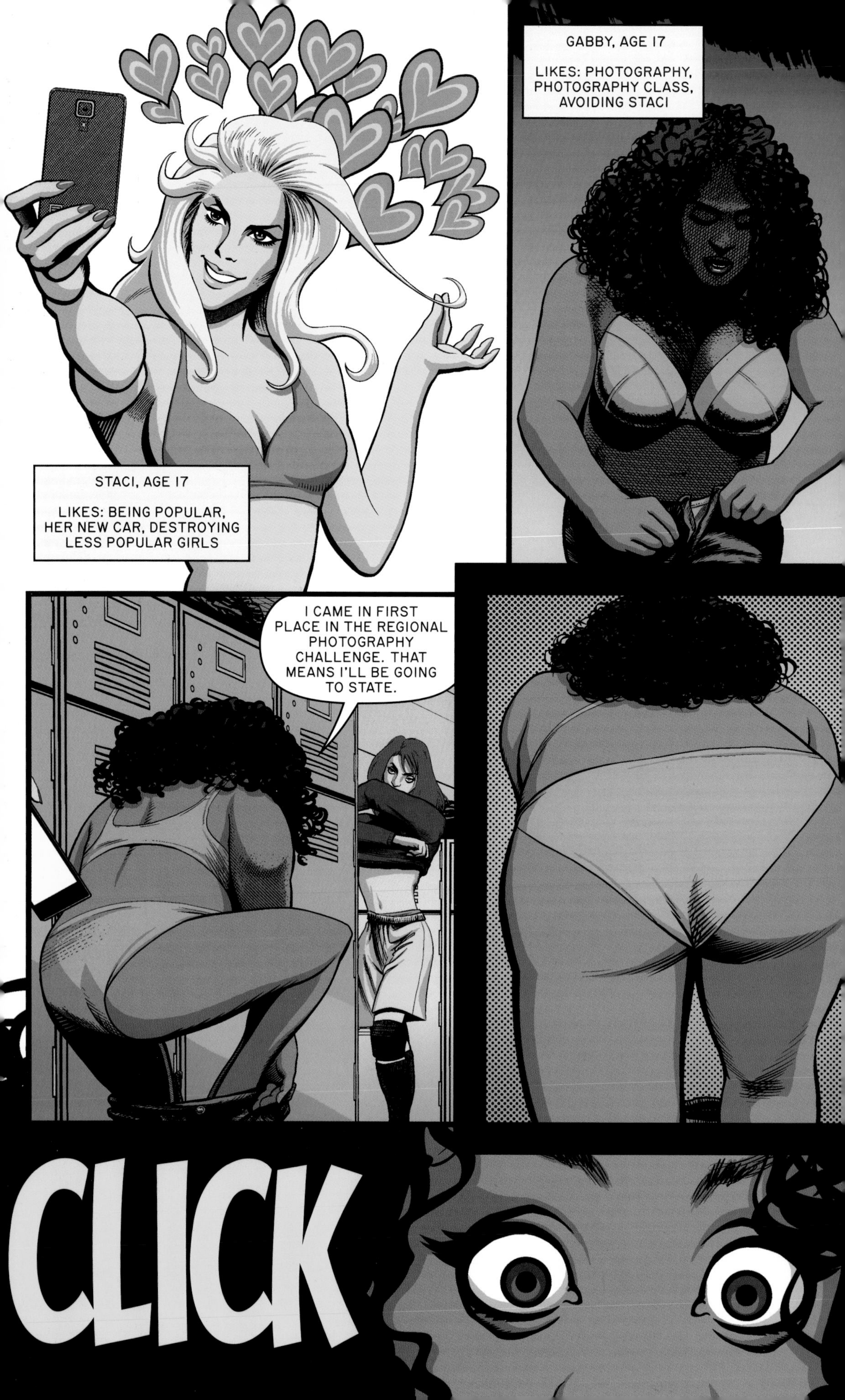
STACI, AGE 17
LIKES: BEING POPULAR, HER NEW CAR, DESTROYING LESS POPULAR GIRLS
GABBY, AGE 17
LIKES: PHOTOGRAPHY, PHOTOGRAPHY CLASS, AVOIDING STACI
I CAME IN FIRST PLACE IN THE REGIONAL PHOTOGRAPHY CHALLENGE. THAT MEANS I'LL BE GOING TO STATE.
CLICK

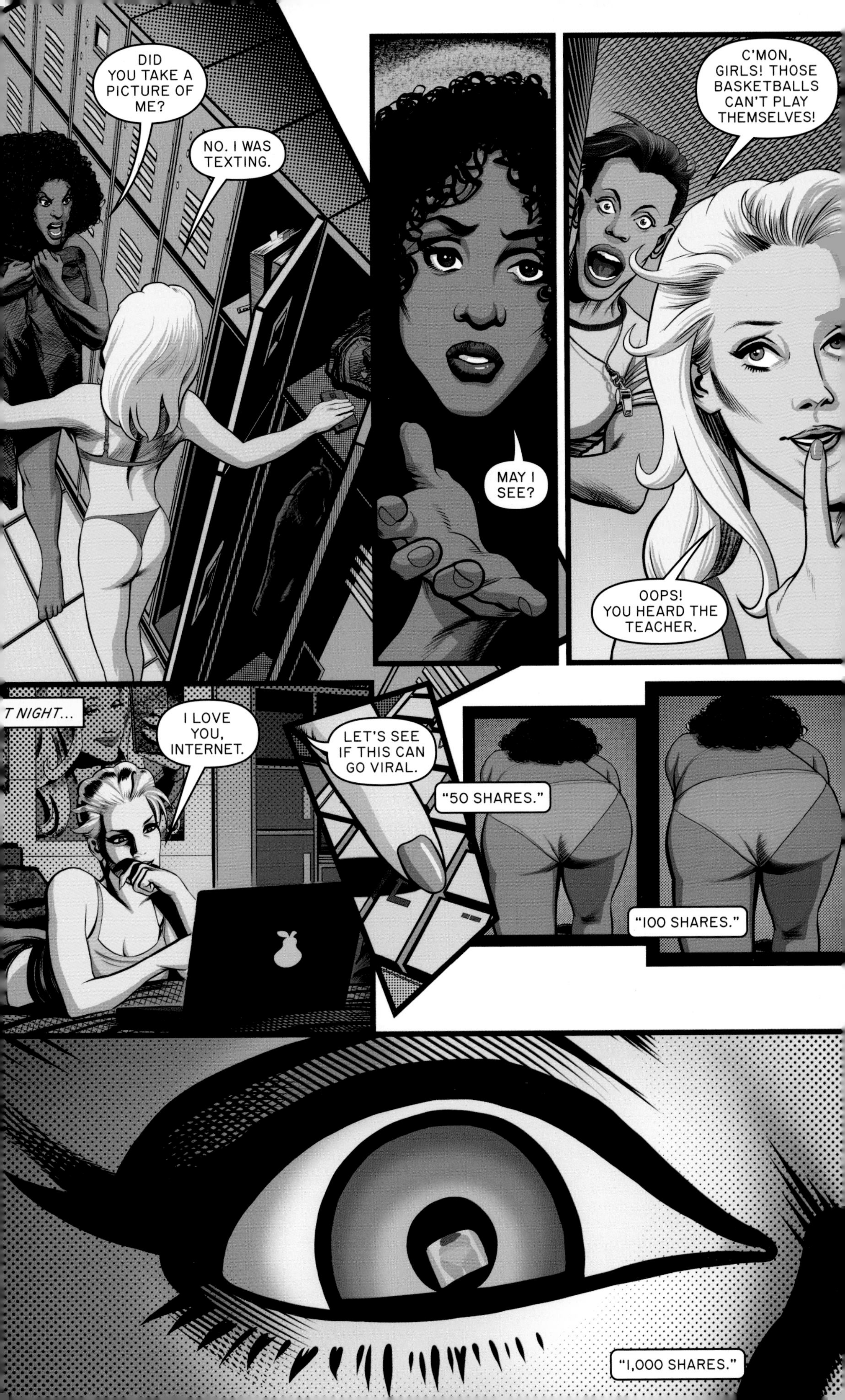
DID YOU TAKE A PICTURE OF ME?
NO. I WAS TEXTING.
MAY I SEE?
C'MON, GIRLS! THOSE BASKETBALLS CAN'T PLAY THEMSELVES!
OOPS! YOU HEARD THE TEACHER.
T NIGHT...
I LOVE YOU, INTERNET.
LET'S SEE IF THIS CAN GO VIRAL.
"50 SHARES."
"100 SHARES."
"1,000 SHARES."

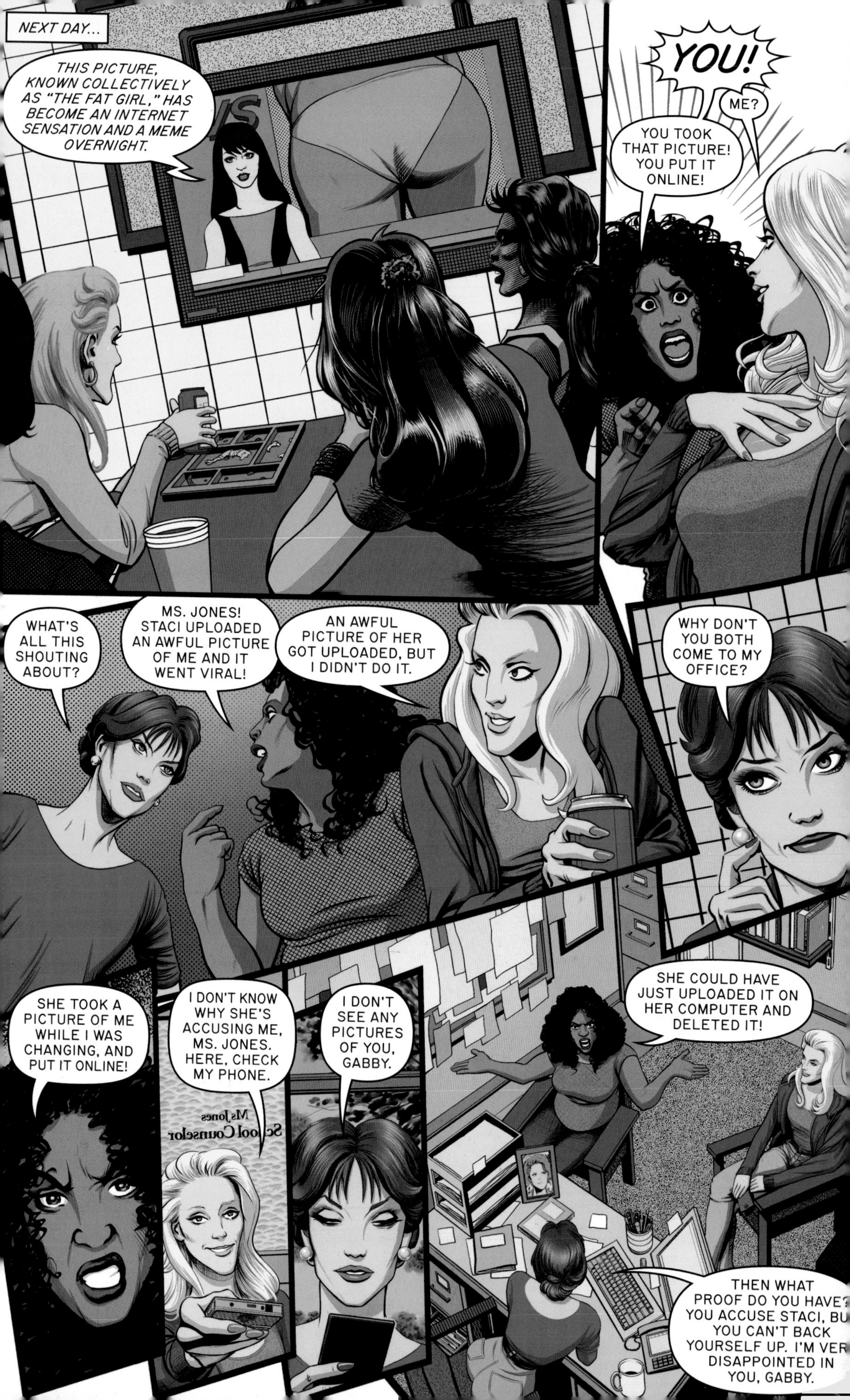
NEXT DAY...
THIS PICTURE, KNOWN COLLECTIVELY AS "THE FAT GIRL," HAS BECOME AN INTERNET SENSATION AND A MEME OVERNIGHT.
YOU!
ME?
YOU TOOK THAT PICTURE! YOU PUT IT ONLINE!
WHAT'S ALL THIS SHOUTING ABOUT?
MS. JONES! STACI UPLOADED AN AWFUL PICTURE OF ME AND IT WENT VIRAL!
AN AWFUL PICTURE OF HER GOT UPLOADED, BUT I DIDN'T DO IT.
WHY DON'T YOU BOTH COME TO MY OFFICE?
SHE TOOK A PICTURE OF ME WHILE I WAS CHANGING, AND PUT IT ONLINE!
I DON'T KNOW WHY SHE'S ACCUSING ME, MS. JONES. HERE, CHECK MY PHONE.
Ms Jones
School Counselor
I DON'T SEE ANY PICTURES OF YOU, GABBY.
SHE COULD HAVE JUST UPLOADED IT ON HER COMPUTER AND DELETED IT!
THEN WHAT PROOF DO YOU HAVE? YOU ACCUSE STACI, BU YOU CAN'T BACK YOURSELF UP. I'M VER DISAPPOINTED IN YOU, GABBY.

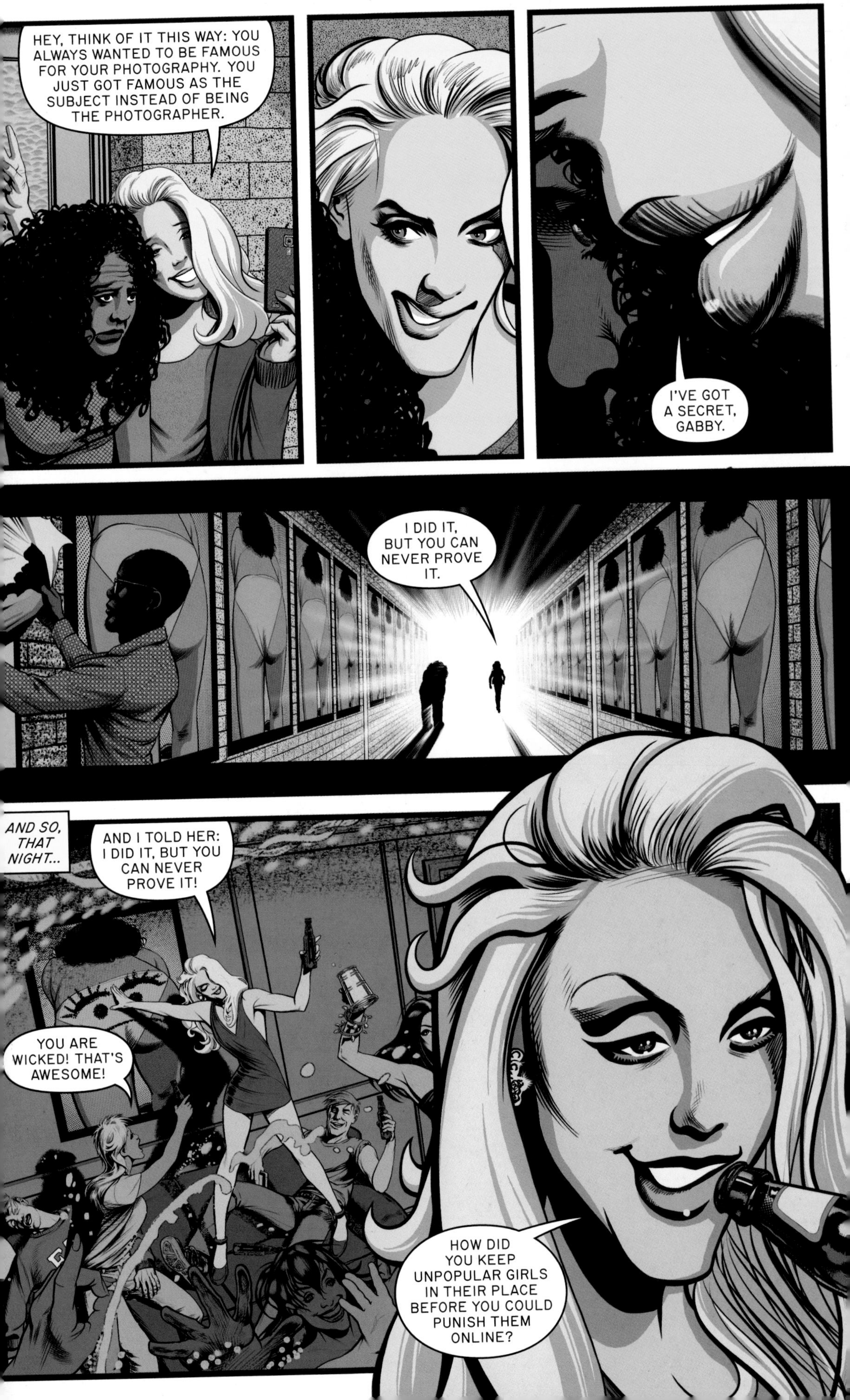
HEY, THINK OF IT THIS WAY: YOU ALWAYS WANTED TO BE FAMOUS FOR YOUR PHOTOGRAPHY. YOU JUST GOT FAMOUS AS THE SUBJECT INSTEAD OF BEING THE PHOTOGRAPHER.
I'VE GOT A SECRET, GABBY.
I DID IT, BUT YOU CAN NEVER PROVE IT.
AND SO, THAT NIGHT...
AND I TOLD HER: I DID IT, BUT YOU CAN NEVER PROVE IT!
YOU ARE WICKED! THAT'S AWESOME!
HOW DID YOU KEEP UNPOPULAR GIRLS IN THEIR PLACE BEFORE YOU COULD PUNISH THEM ONLINE?

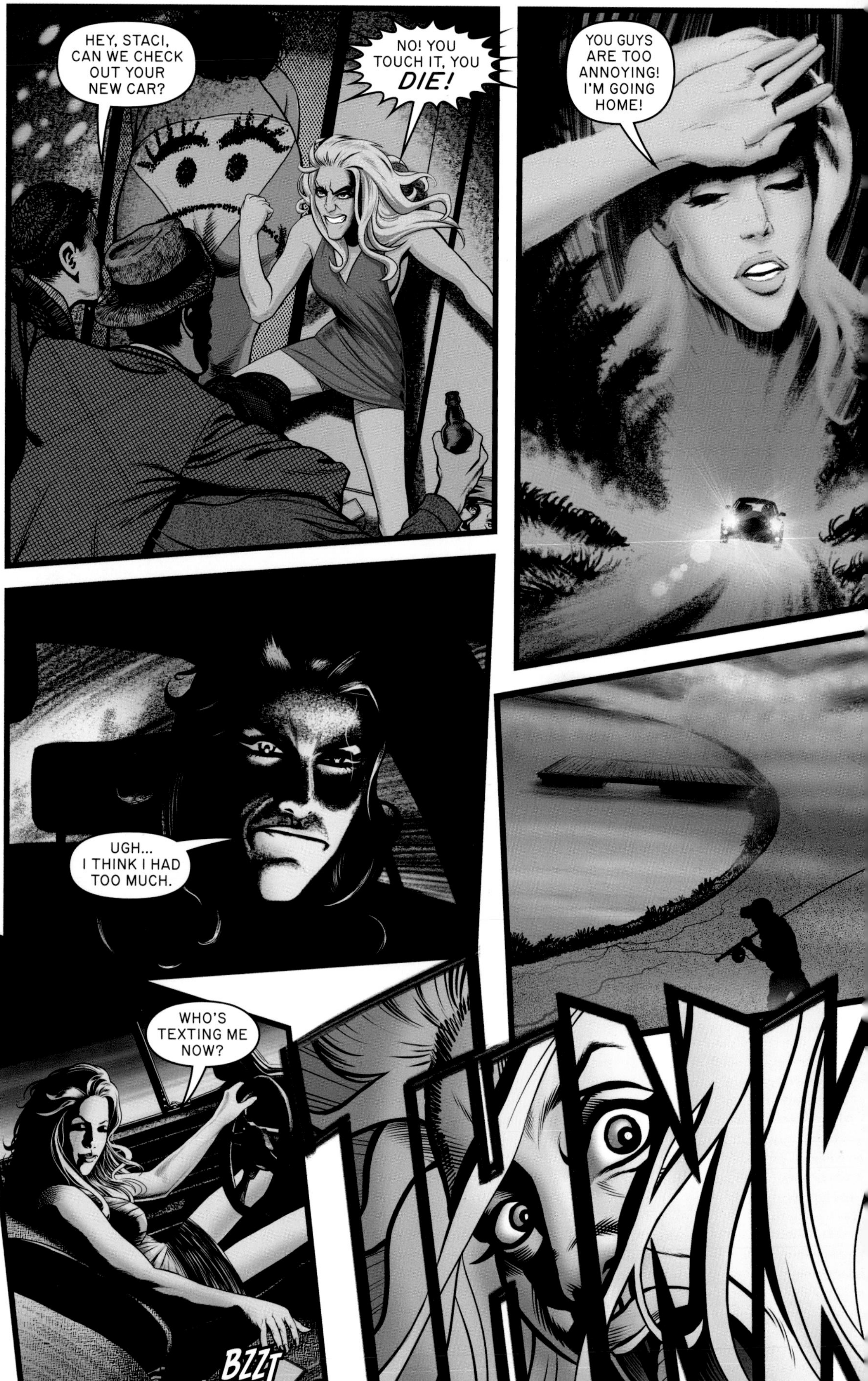
HEY, STACI, CAN WE CHECK OUT YOUR NEW CAR?
NO! YOU TOUCH IT, YOU DIE!
YOU GUYS ARE TOO ANNOYING! I'M GOING HOME!
UGH... I THINK I HAD TOO MUCH.
WHO'S TEXTING ME NOW?
BZZT

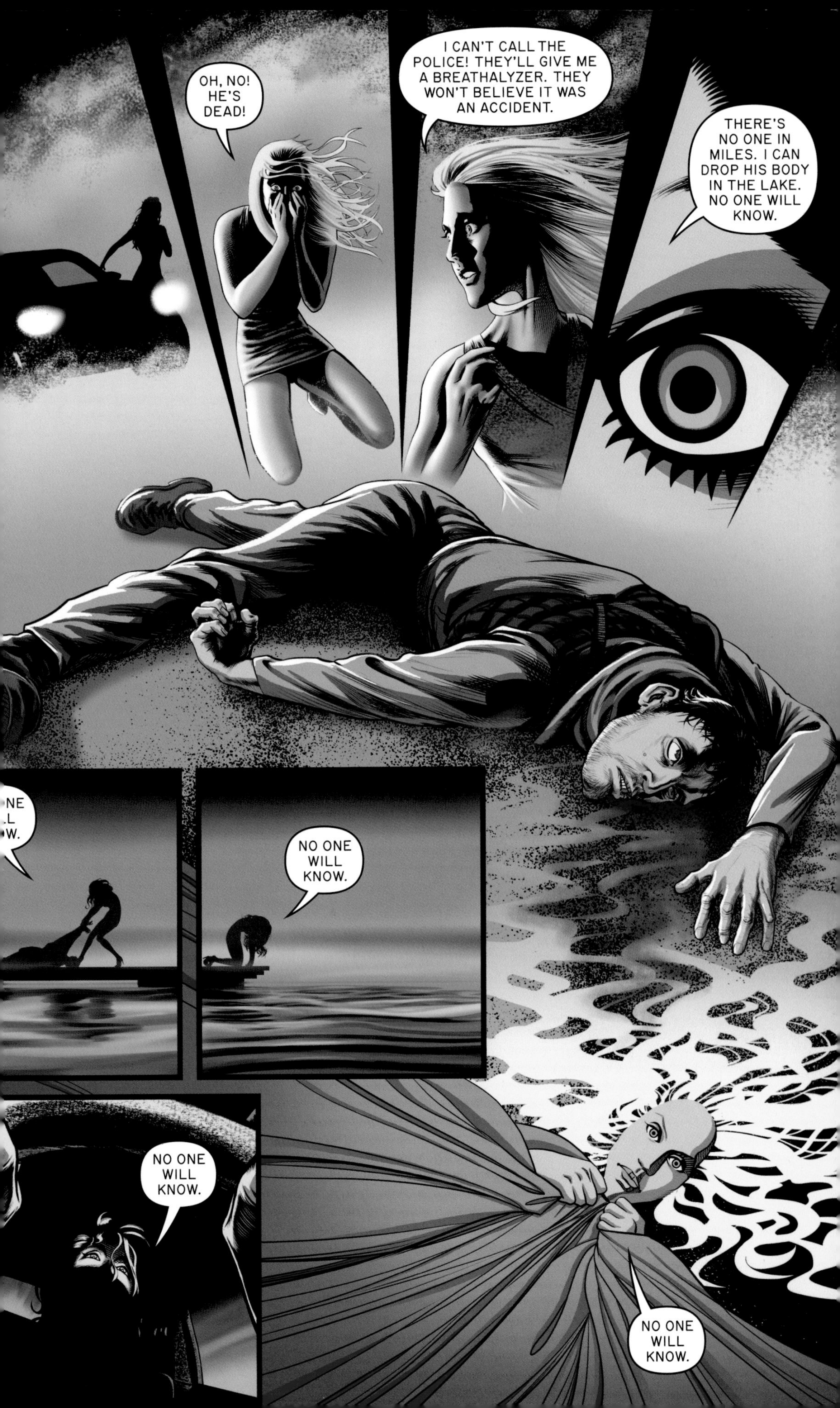
OH, NO! HE'S DEAD!
I CAN'T CALL THE POLICE! THEY'LL GIVE ME A BREATHALYZER. THEY WON'T BELIEVE IT WAS AN ACCIDENT.
THERE'S NO ONE IN MILES. I CAN DROP HIS BODY IN THE LAKE. NO ONE WILL KNOW.
NO ONE WILL KNOW.
NO ONE WILL KNOW.
NO ONE WILL KNOW.

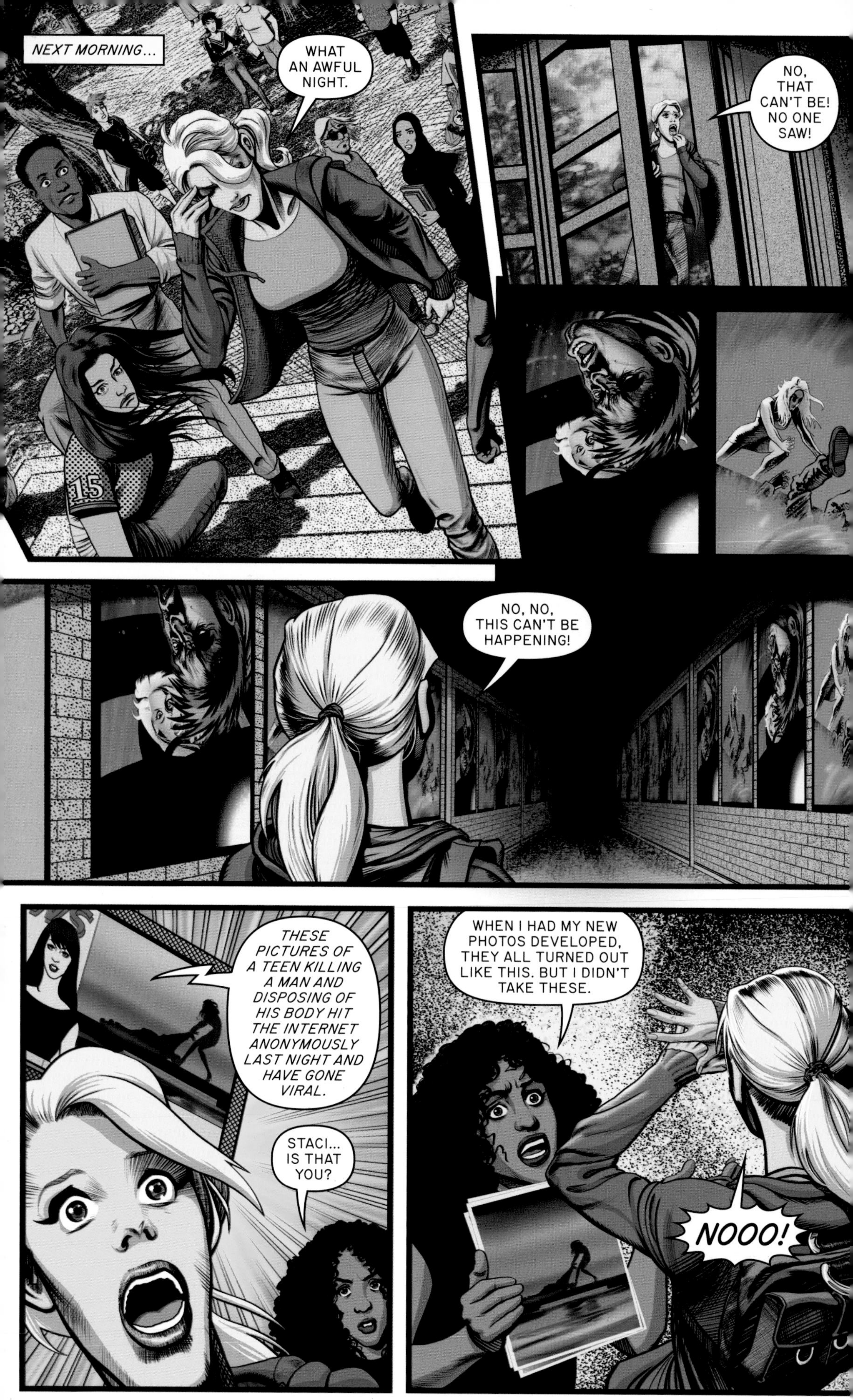

NEXT MORNING...
WHAT AN AWFUL NIGHT.
NO, THAT CAN'T BE! NO ONE SAW!
NO, NO, THIS CAN'T BE HAPPENING!
THESE PICTURES OF A TEEN KILLING A MAN AND DISPOSING OF HIS BODY HIT THE INTERNET ANONYMOUSLY LAST NIGHT AND HAVE GONE VIRAL.
STACI... IS THAT YOU?
WHEN I HAD MY NEW PHOTOS DEVELOPED, THEY ALL TURNED OUT LIKE THIS. BUT I DIDN'T TAKE THESE.
NOOO!

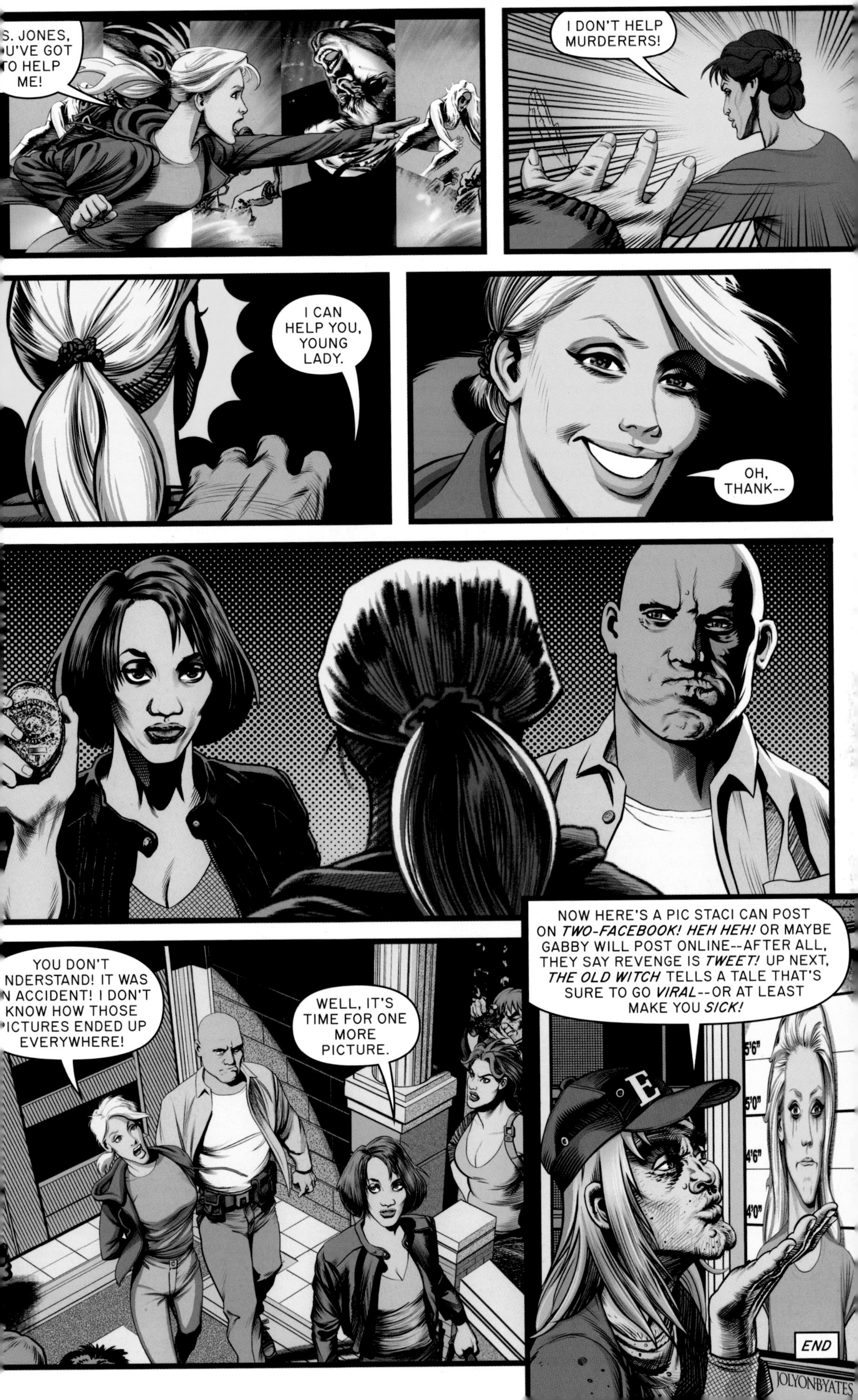
S. JONES, U'VE GOT O HELP ME!
I DON'T HELP MURDERERS!
I CAN HELP YOU, YOUNG LADY.
OH, THANK--
YOU DON'T NDERSTAND! IT WAS N ACCIDENT! I DON'T KNOW HOW THOSE ICTURES ENDED UP EVERYWHERE!
WELL, IT'S TIME FOR ONE MORE PICTURE.
NOW HERE'S A PIC STACI CAN POST ON *TWO-FACEBOOK! HEH HEH!* OR MAYBE GABBY WILL POST ONLINE--AFTER ALL, THEY SAY REVENGE IS *TWEET!* UP NEXT, *THE OLD WITCH* TELLS A TALE THAT'S SURE TO GO *VIRAL*--OR AT LEAST MAKE YOU *SICK!*
5'6"
5'0"
4'6"
4'0"
E
END
JOLYONBYATES

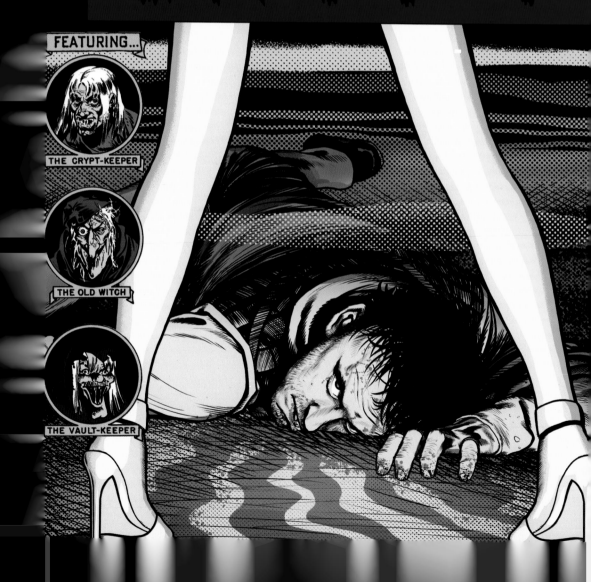

NEW STORIES BY DAVIDSON, YATES, BLANCH, KIM, AND LOST CLASSICS BY <u>BERNIE WRIGHTSON!</u>

 AN ENTERTAINING COMIC

SUPER GENIUS

TERROR

NO. 2
$3.99 US
$5.50 CAN

TALES FROM THE CRYPT

FEATURING...

THE CRYPT-KEEPER

THE OLD WITCH

THE VAULT-KEEPER

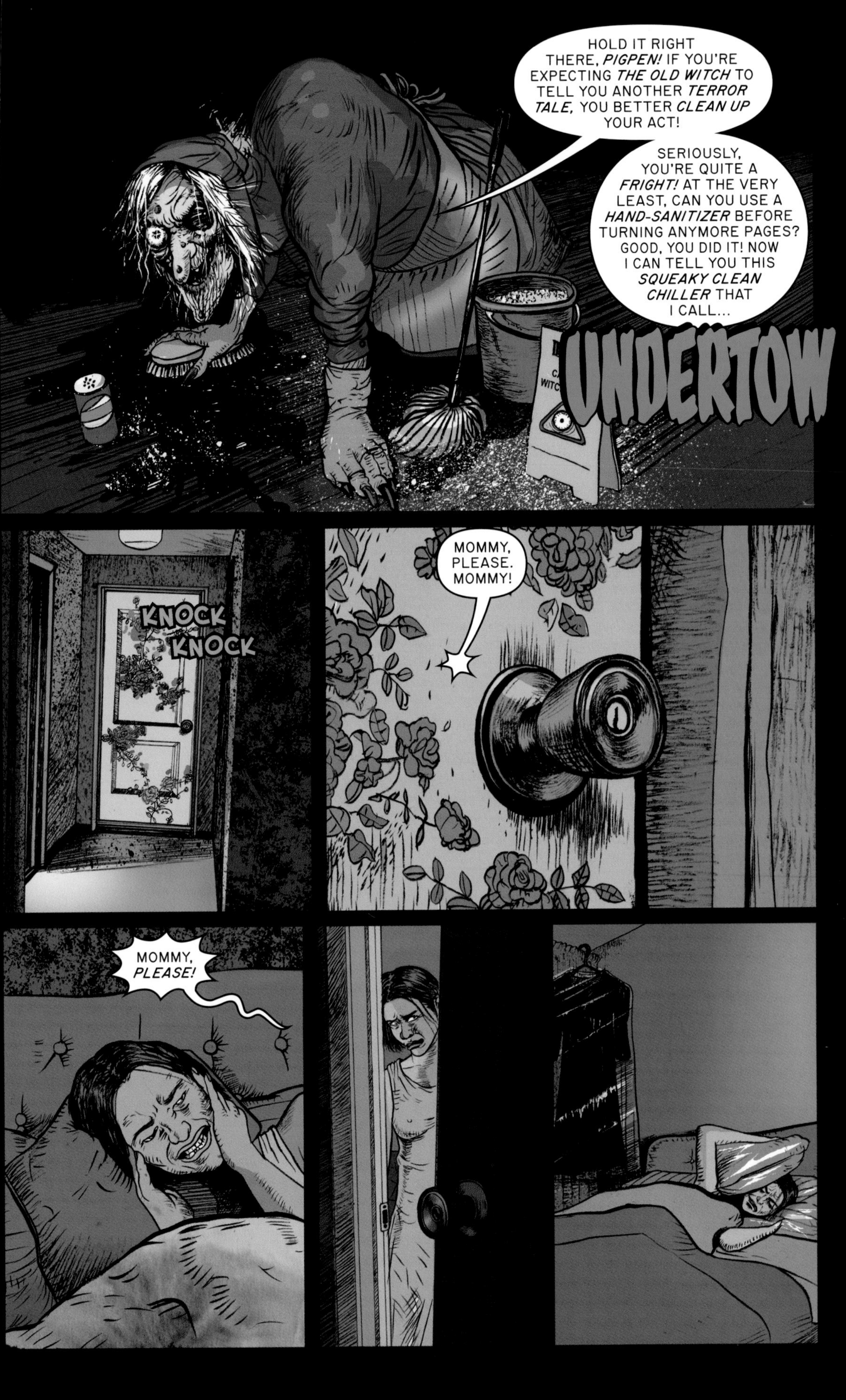
HOLD IT RIGHT THERE, *PIGPEN!* IF YOU'RE EXPECTING *THE OLD WITCH* TO TELL YOU ANOTHER *TERROR TALE,* YOU BETTER *CLEAN UP* YOUR ACT!
SERIOUSLY, YOU'RE QUITE A *FRIGHT!* AT THE VERY LEAST, CAN YOU USE A *HAND-SANITIZER* BEFORE TURNING ANYMORE PAGES? GOOD, YOU DID IT! NOW I CAN TELL YOU THIS *SQUEAKY CLEAN CHILLER* THAT I CALL...
UNDERTOW
KNOCK KNOCK
MOMMY, PLEASE. MOMMY!
MOMMY, *PLEASE!*

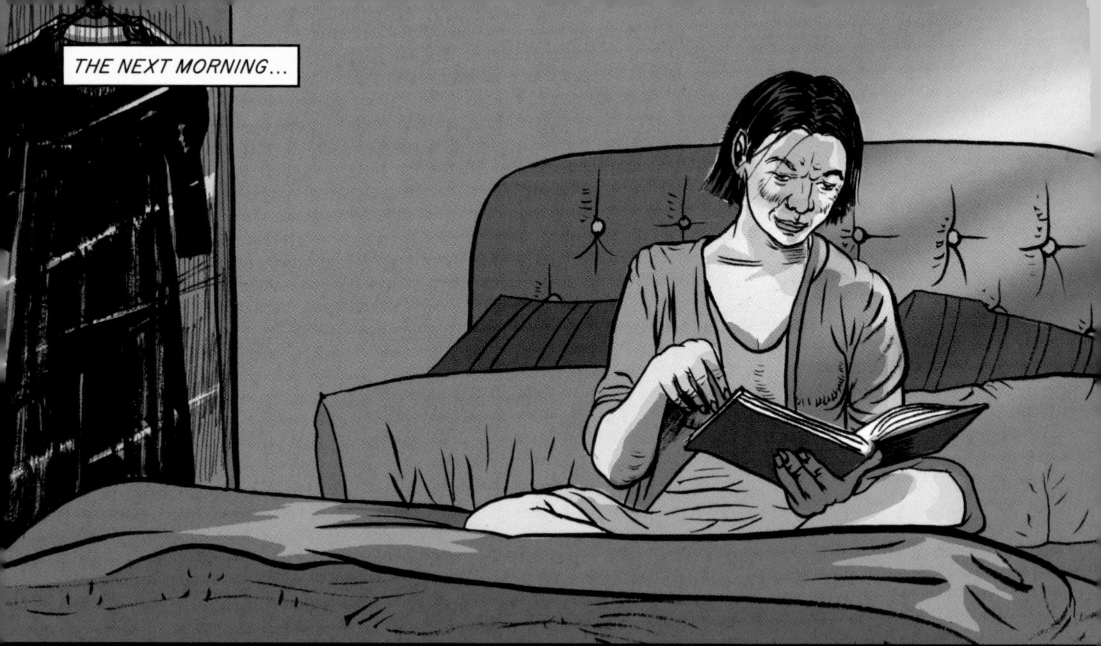
THE NEXT MORNING…

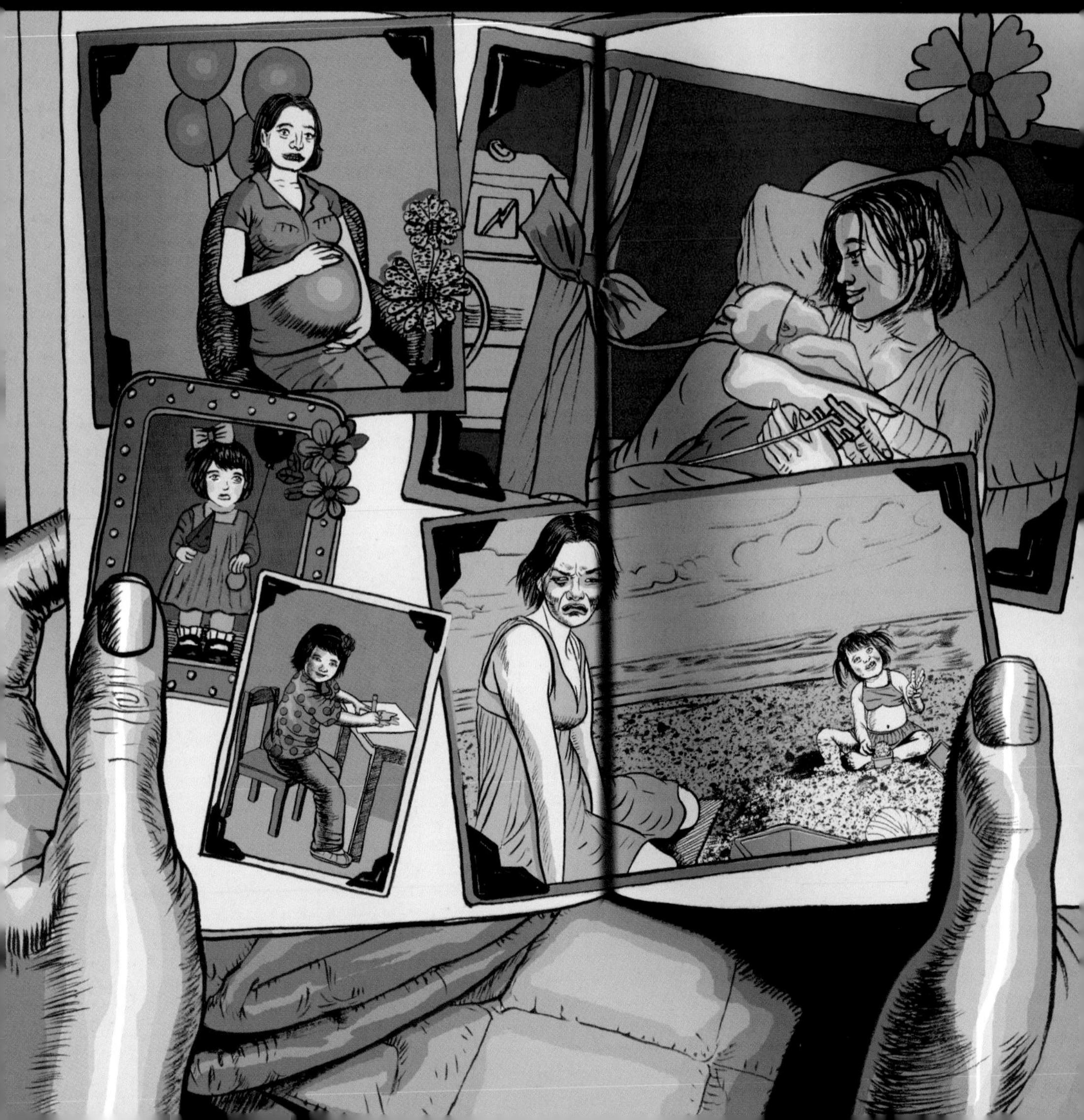

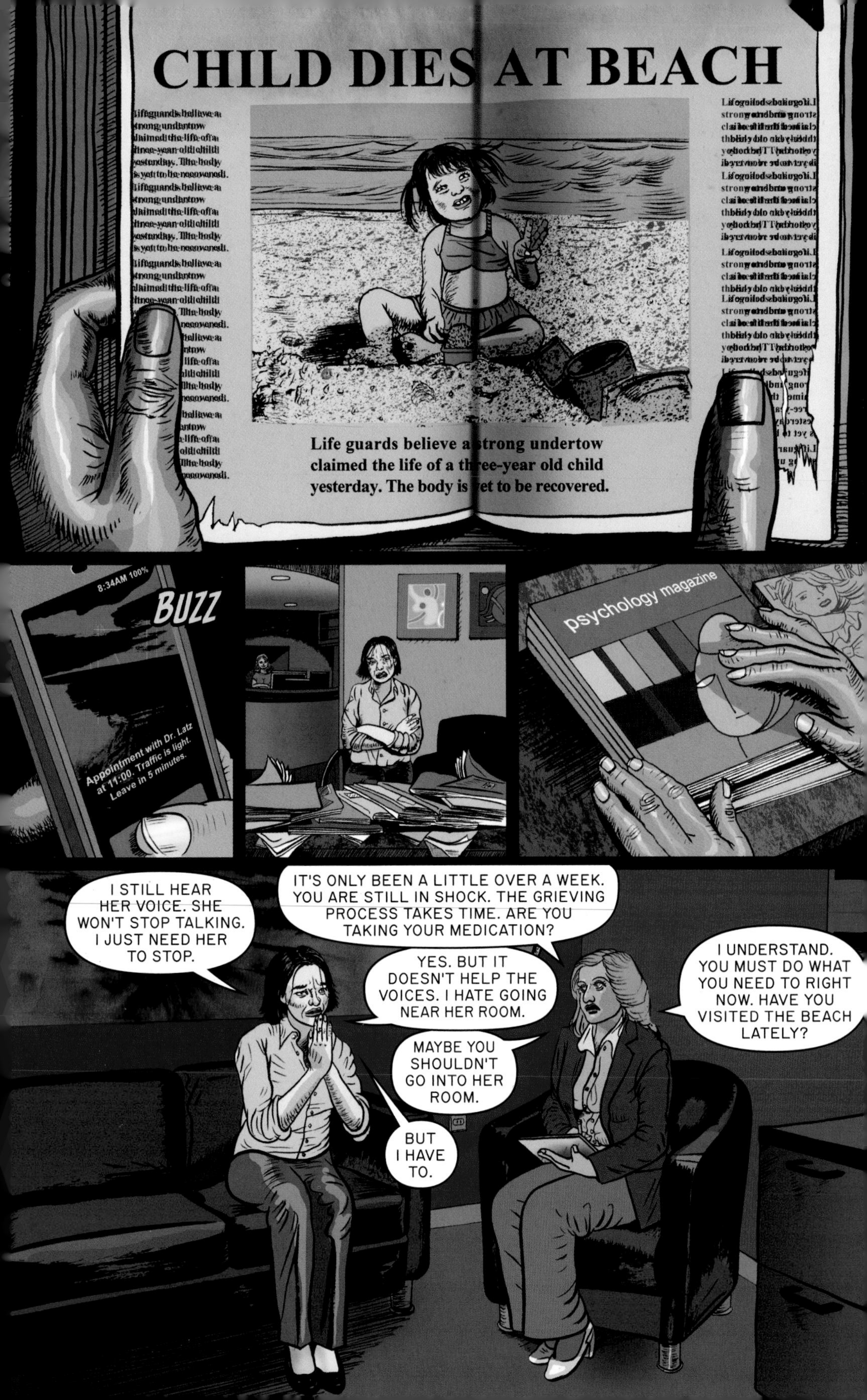
CHILD DIES AT BEACH
Life guards believe a strong undertow claimed the life of a three-year old child yesterday. The body is yet to be recovered.
8:34AM 100%
BUZZ
Appointment with Dr. Latz at 11:00. Traffic is light. Leave in 5 minutes.
psychology magazine
I STILL HEAR HER VOICE. SHE WON'T STOP TALKING. I JUST NEED HER TO STOP.
IT'S ONLY BEEN A LITTLE OVER A WEEK. YOU ARE STILL IN SHOCK. THE GRIEVING PROCESS TAKES TIME. ARE YOU TAKING YOUR MEDICATION?
YES. BUT IT DOESN'T HELP THE VOICES. I HATE GOING NEAR HER ROOM.
MAYBE YOU SHOULDN'T GO INTO HER ROOM.
BUT I HAVE TO.
I UNDERSTAND. YOU MUST DO WHAT YOU NEED TO RIGHT NOW. HAVE YOU VISITED THE BEACH LATELY?

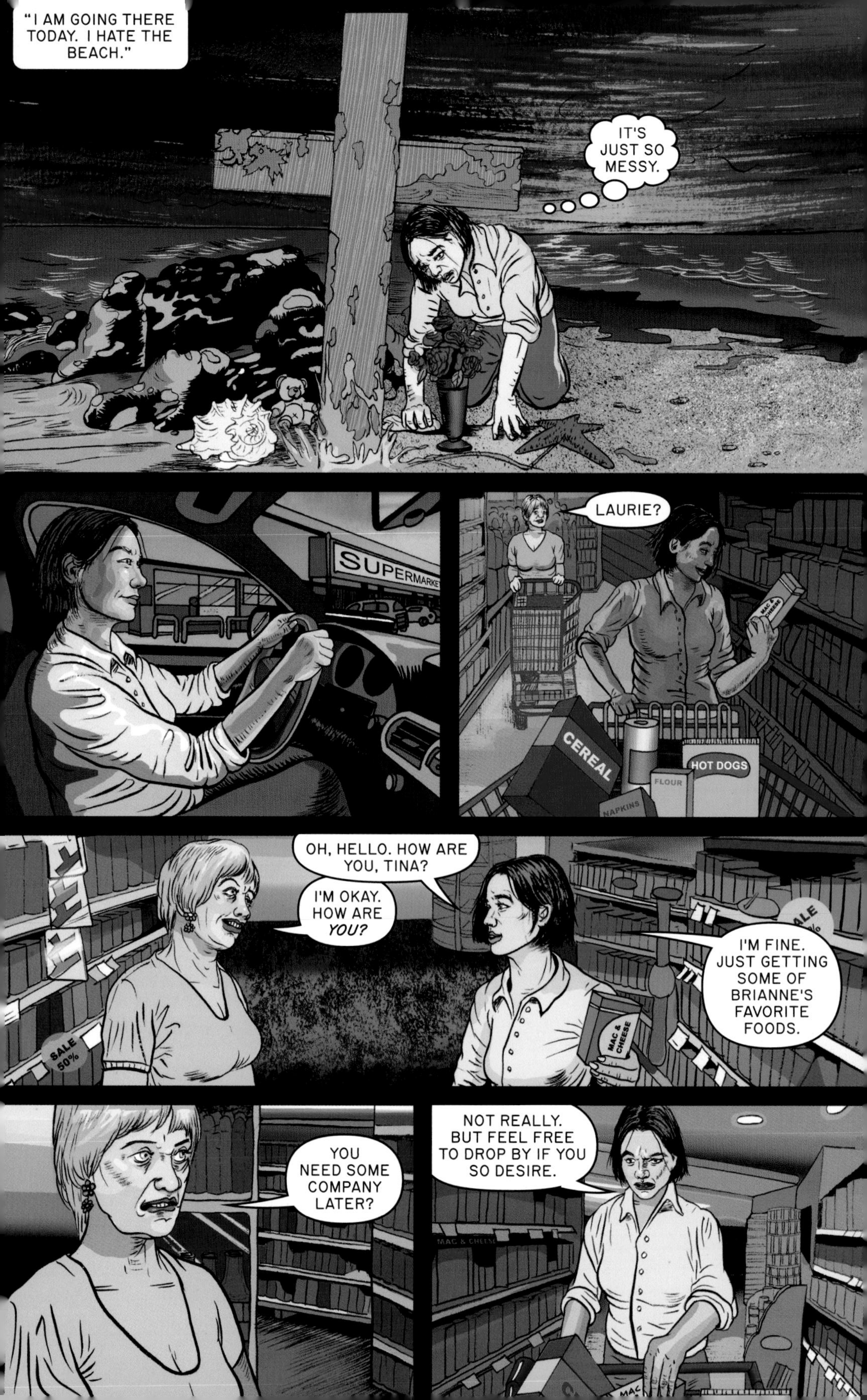
"I AM GOING THERE TODAY. I HATE THE BEACH."
IT'S JUST SO MESSY.
SUPERMARKET
LAURIE?
MAC & CHEESE
CEREAL
HOT DOGS
FLOUR
NAPKINS
OH, HELLO. HOW ARE YOU, TINA?
I'M OKAY. HOW ARE *YOU?*
I'M FINE. JUST GETTING SOME OF BRIANNE'S FAVORITE FOODS.
SALE 50%
MAC & CHEESE
YOU NEED SOME COMPANY LATER?
NOT REALLY. BUT FEEL FREE TO DROP BY IF YOU SO DESIRE.
MAC & CHEESE

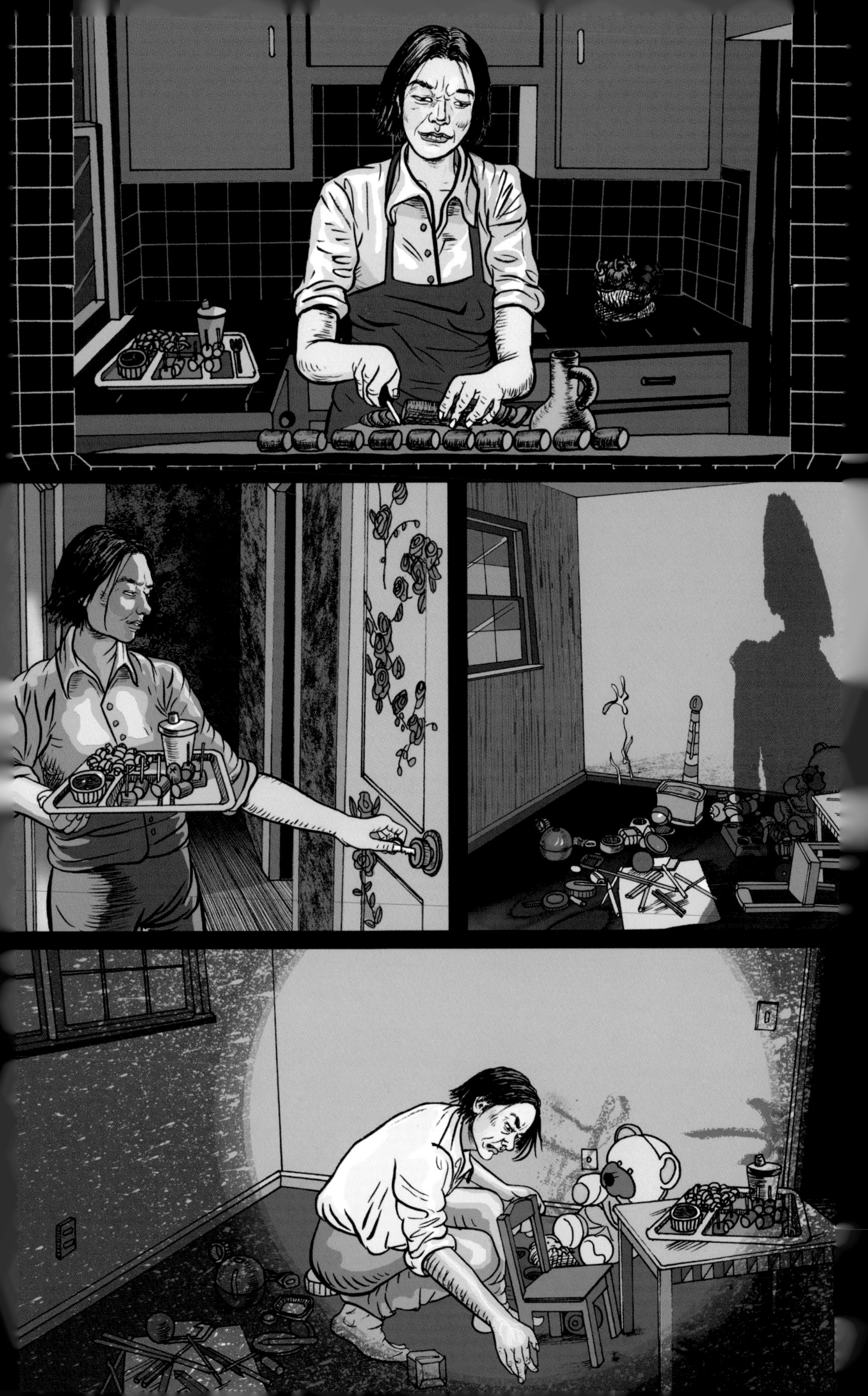

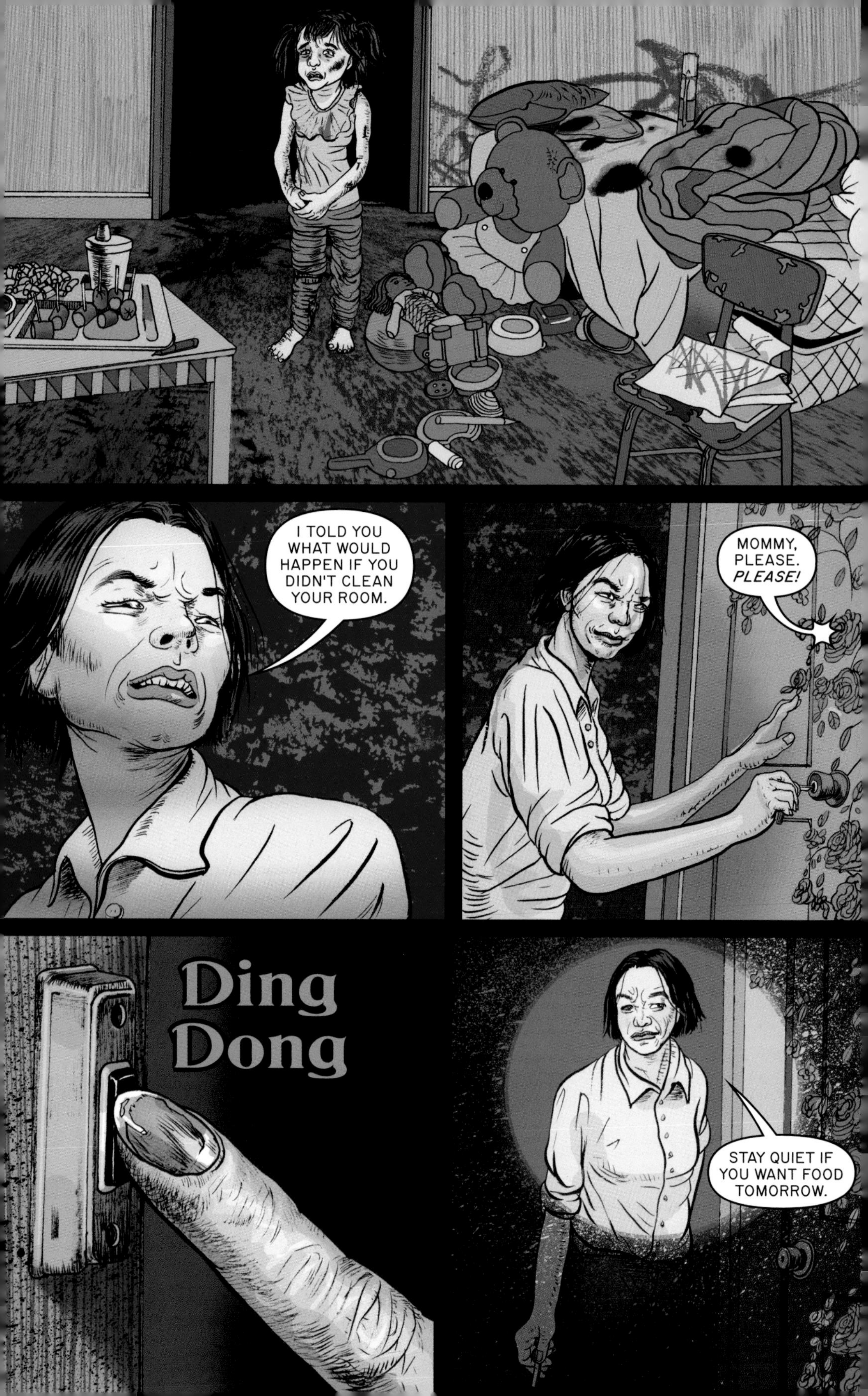
I TOLD YOU WHAT WOULD HAPPEN IF YOU DIDN'T CLEAN YOUR ROOM.
MOMMY, PLEASE. *PLEASE!*
Ding Dong
STAY QUIET IF YOU WANT FOOD TOMORROW.

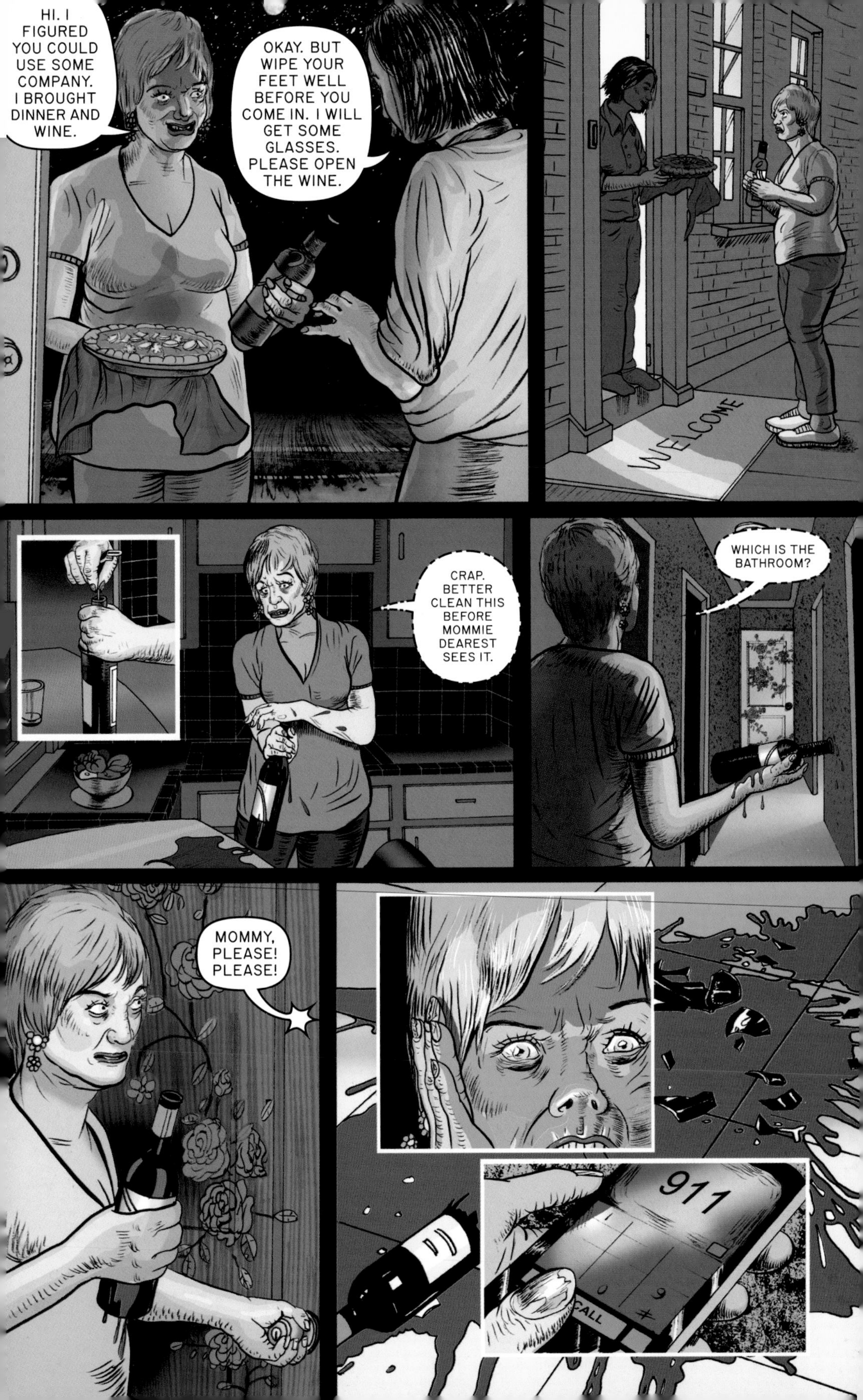
HI. I FIGURED YOU COULD USE SOME COMPANY. I BROUGHT DINNER AND WINE.
OKAY. BUT WIPE YOUR FEET WELL BEFORE YOU COME IN. I WILL GET SOME GLASSES. PLEASE OPEN THE WINE.
WELCOME
CRAP. BETTER CLEAN THIS BEFORE MOMMIE DEAREST SEES IT.
WHICH IS THE BATHROOM?
MOMMY, PLEASE! PLEASE!
911
CALL

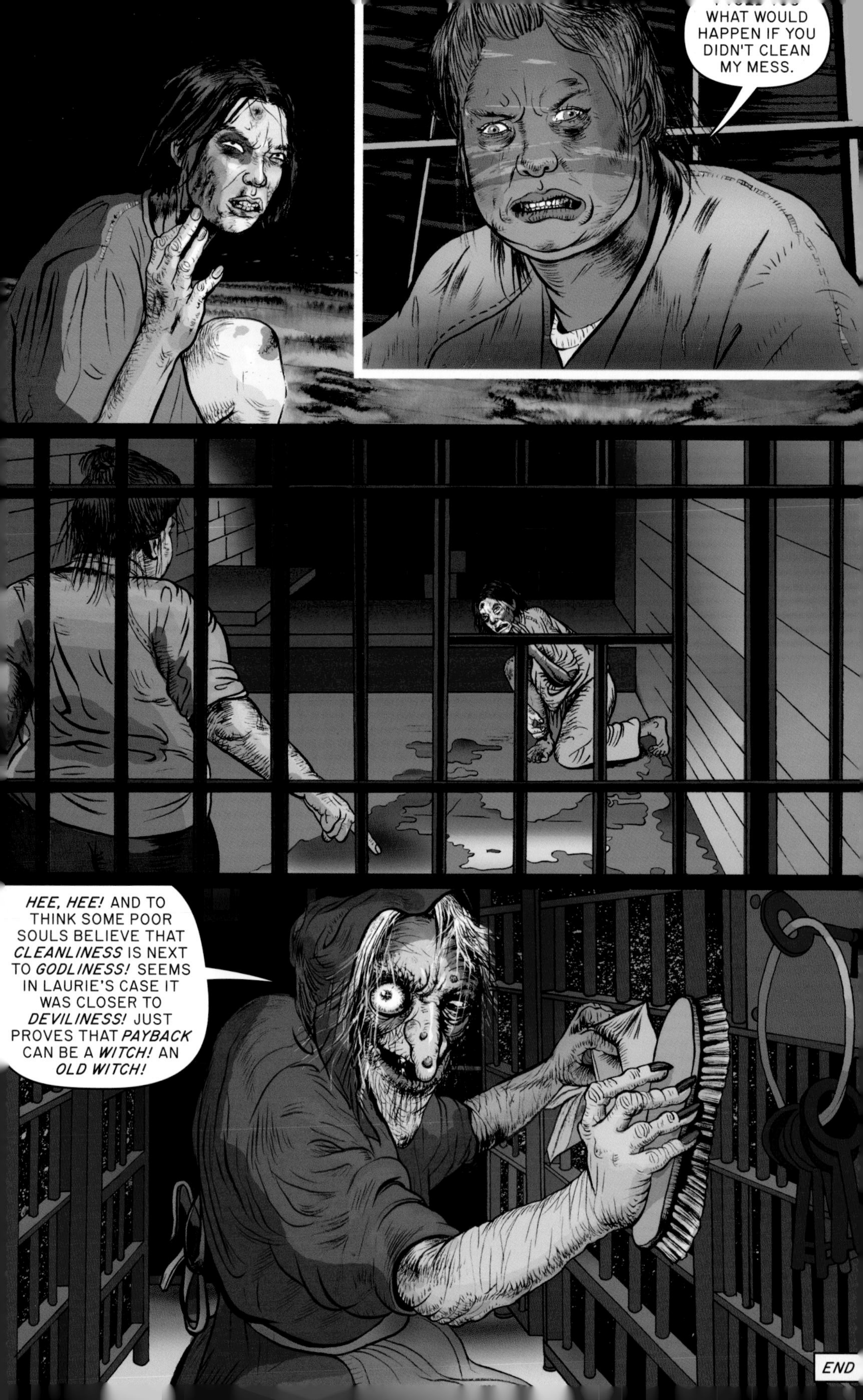
WHAT WOULD HAPPEN IF YOU DIDN'T CLEAN MY MESS.
HEE, HEE! AND TO THINK SOME POOR SOULS BELIEVE THAT CLEANLINESS IS NEXT TO GODLINESS! SEEMS IN LAURIE'S CASE IT WAS CLOSER TO DEVILINESS! JUST PROVES THAT PAYBACK CAN BE A WITCH! AN OLD WITCH!
END

THE VAULT OF HORROR!®

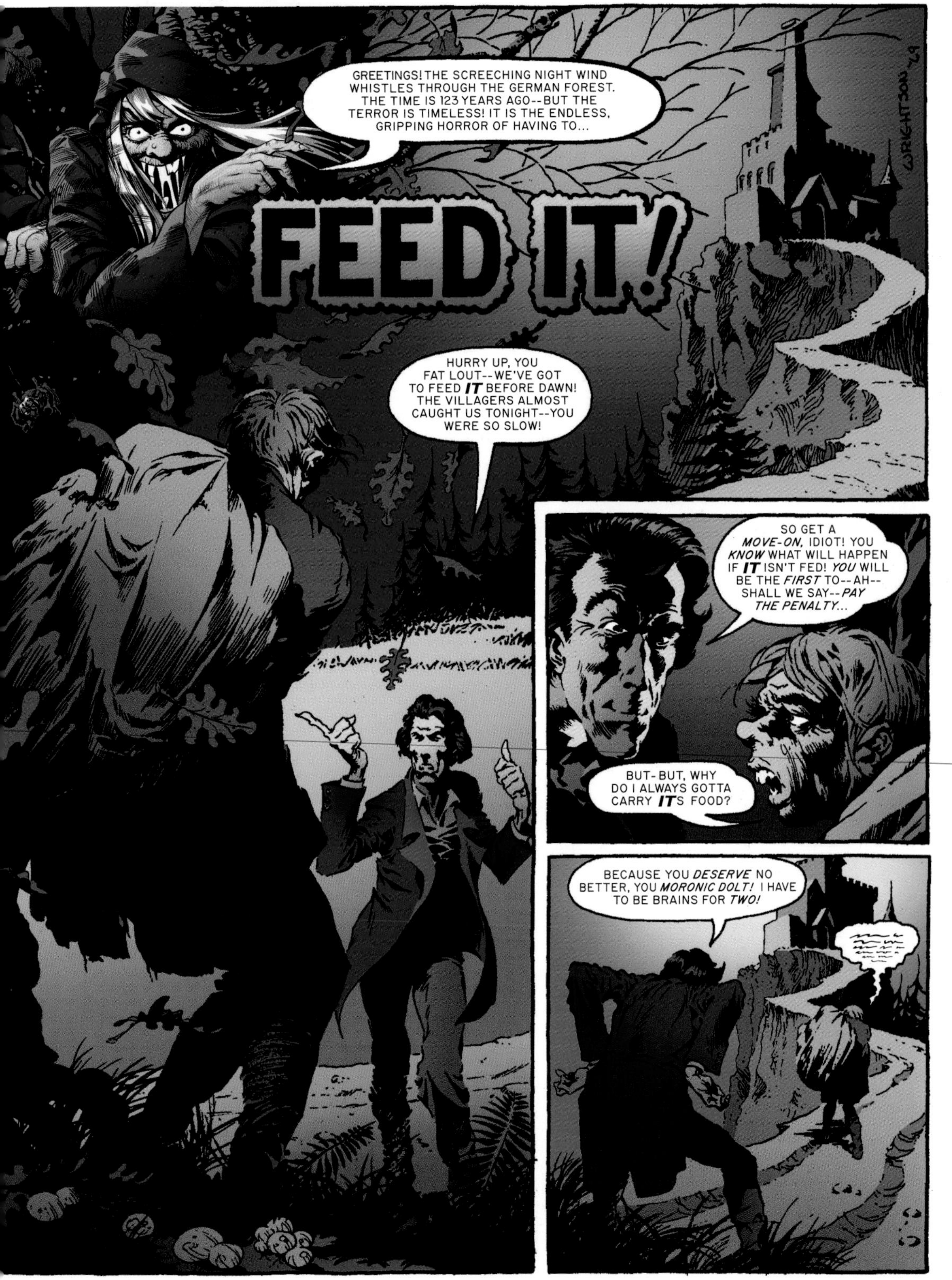
GREETINGS! THE SCREECHING NIGHT WIND WHISTLES THROUGH THE GERMAN FOREST. THE TIME IS 123 YEARS AGO--BUT THE TERROR IS TIMELESS! IT IS THE ENDLESS, GRIPPING HORROR OF HAVING TO...
FEED IT!
HURRY UP, YOU FAT LOUT--WE'VE GOT TO FEED IT BEFORE DAWN! THE VILLAGERS ALMOST CAUGHT US TONIGHT--YOU WERE SO SLOW!
SO GET A MOVE-ON, IDIOT! YOU KNOW WHAT WILL HAPPEN IF IT ISN'T FED! YOU WILL BE THE FIRST TO--AH--SHALL WE SAY--PAY THE PENALTY...
BUT-BUT, WHY DO I ALWAYS GOTTA CARRY ITS FOOD?
BECAUSE YOU DESERVE NO BETTER, YOU MORONIC DOLT! I HAVE TO BE BRAINS FOR TWO!

I WAS THE ONE WHO FOUND **IT**--AND LURED **IT** UP FROM THE FEN--AND I HAD THE INTELLIGENCE TO FIGURE OUT HOW TO *USE* THE *VILLAGE* TO TAKE *CARE* OF **IT**-- *CHEAP!*

SO WHEN I SAY "FEED **IT**." I *MEAN* "FEED **IT!**"

BUT-BUT I GET THE *SHIVERS* JUST *LOOKIN'* AT THIS HORRIBLE PLACE--IT'S SO *DARK*--AND-AND *GLOOMY*, AND--

STOP YOUR CRYING! **IT** NEEDS DAMPNESS AND DARK AS *WELL* AS FOOD! AND WE *MUST* KEEP **IT** ALIVE!

BUT-BUT...

SHUT UP! THE AMERICAN CIRC PROMOTER WILL PAY ME *WELL* F **IT**! I WILL NOT PASS *THAT* UP FOR *YOUR* WEAK STOMACH!

NOW, *MOVE*, YOU FAT SNAIL!

AH, POOR JOSEF--HOW *TERRIBLE* TO BE SADDLED WITH SUCH AN *INCOMPETENT* ON THE EVE OF YOUR GREATEST OPPORTUNITY! BUT, DOESN'T THE *STALE AIR SHIVER* YOUR SNEERING NOSTRILS?

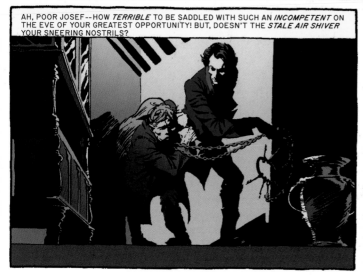

DOESN'T THE *DUST* SEEM TO *TINGLE* WITH WARNING? DON'T YOU *FEEL* YOUR SKIN *GRATE* AS THE *DUNGEON DOOR* CREAKS OPEN?

THE *DUNGEON*-- IN DAYS GONE BY, THE SITE OF DEEDS OF *UNSPEAKABLE HORROR*... NOW, A *CATCH-ALL* FOR THE UNUSED, BROKEN AND TIME-WORN... BUT, DOESN'T THE CENTURIES-OLD *FEAR* CRAWL THROUGH YOU WHEN *FATE* TAKES A HAND IN YOUR LIFE?

OOF!

WHA--!?!

NO-NO! YOU-YOU *COULDN'T!* YOU- TH-THIS IS--*TERRIBLE!!*

THAT'S THE ONLY THING *IT* WILL *EAT!* SO HELP ME, IF YOU KILLED...

N'T YOU FEEL *DESTINY* WORKING AGAINST YOU WHEN YOU RIP OPEN UR PRECIOUS SACK AND DISCOVER...

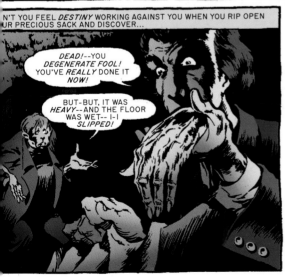

DEAD!--YOU *DEGENERATE FOOL!* YOU'VE *REALLY* DONE IT *NOW!*

BUT-BUT, IT WAS *HEAVY*--AND THE FLOOR WAS WET-- I-I *SLIPPED!*

BUT, IT HAD BEEN *ALIVE!* *IT* NEEDS A LIVE BODY TO EAT!

THERE IS ONLY *ONE CHANCE*-- YOU!

BUT-BUT-- WE CAN GO GET ANOTHER ONE!

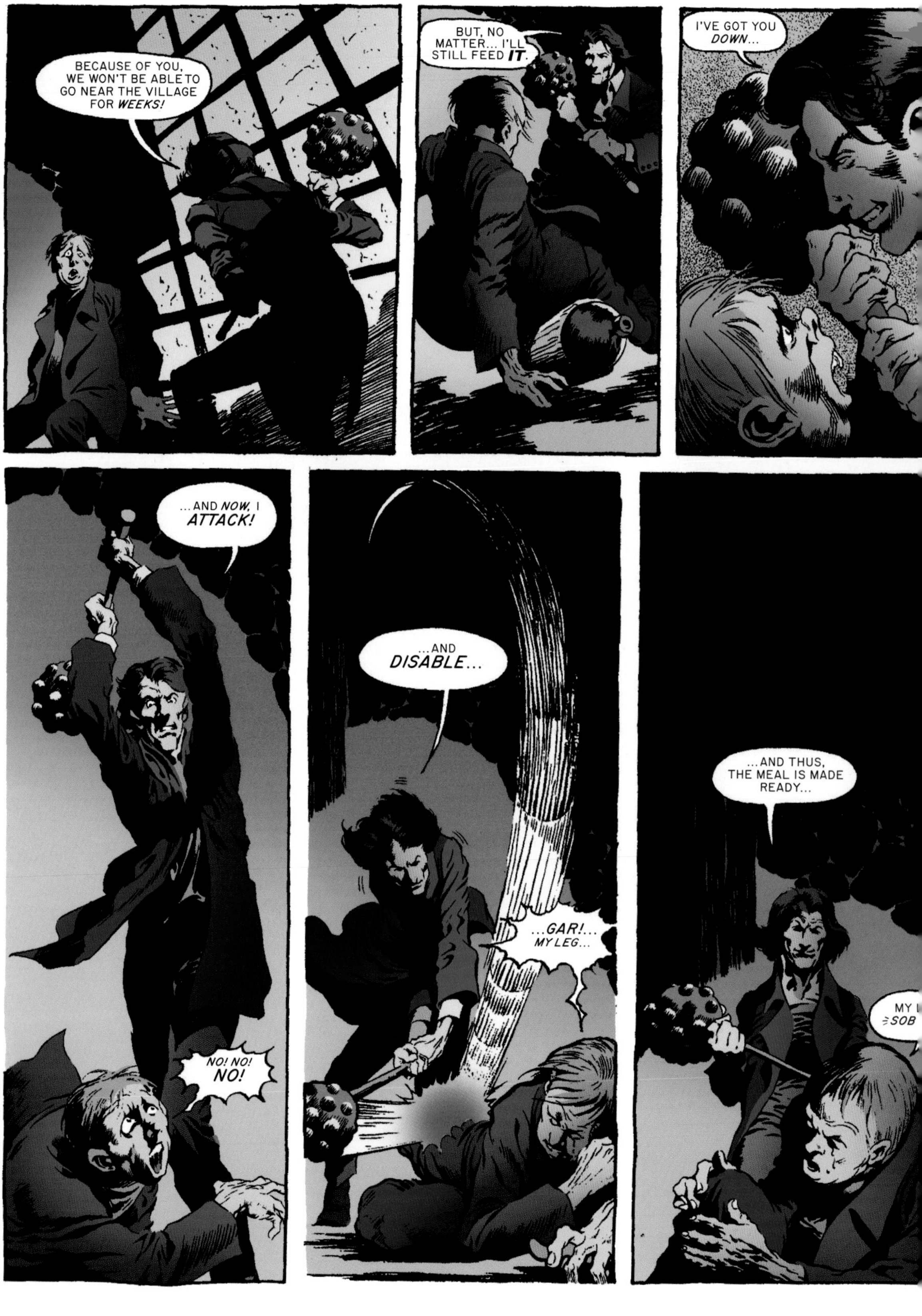

BECAUSE OF YOU, WE WON'T BE ABLE TO GO NEAR THE VILLAGE FOR *WEEKS!*
BUT, NO MATTER... I'LL STILL FEED ***IT***.
I'VE GOT YOU *DOWN*...
...AND *NOW*, I *ATTACK!*
NO! NO! NO!
...AND *DISABLE*...
...GAR!... MY LEG...
...AND THUS, THE MEAL IS MADE READY...
MY
SOB

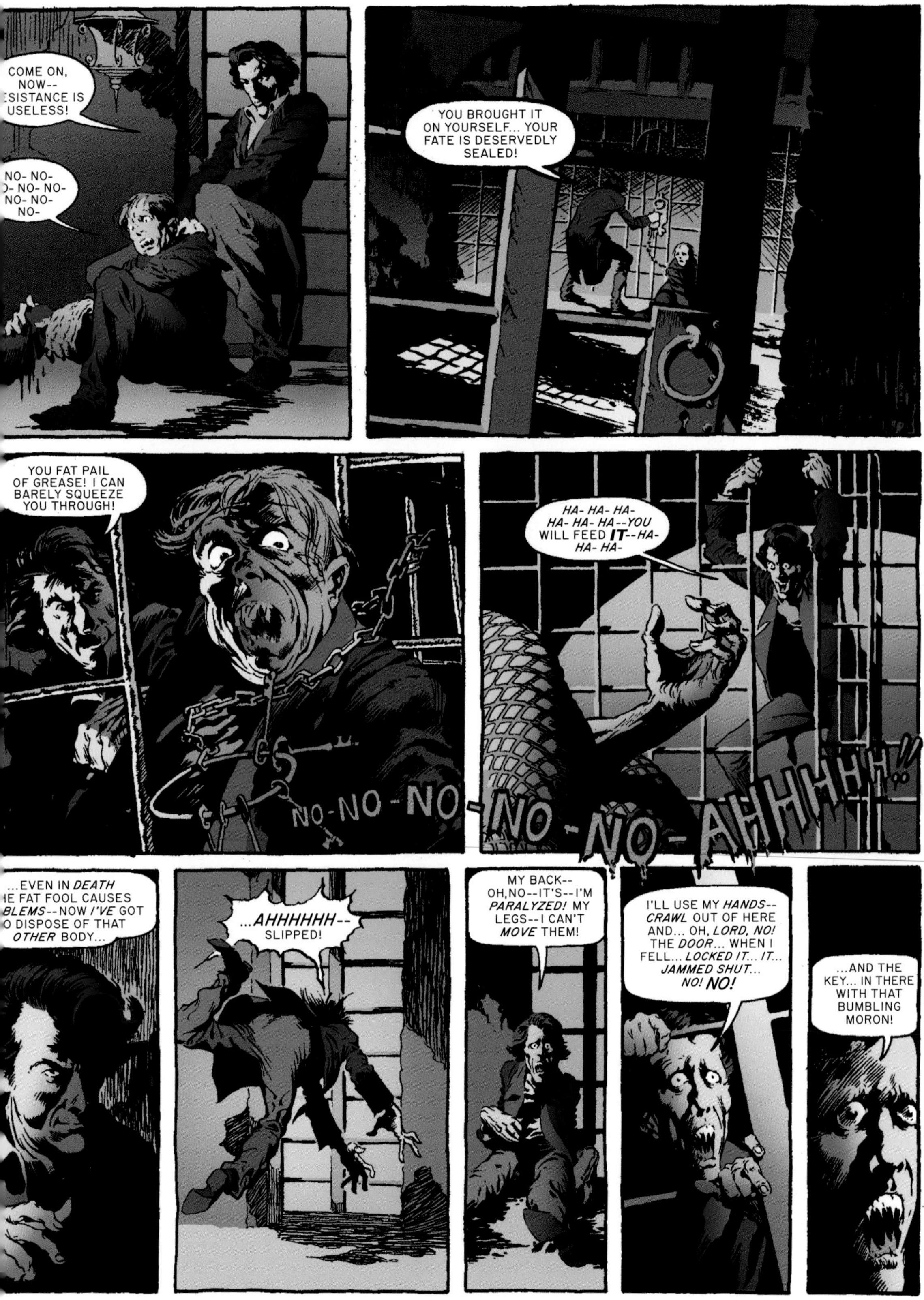

COME ON, NOW-- :SISTANCE IS USELESS!
NO- NO-)- NO- NO- NO- NO- NO-
YOU BROUGHT IT ON YOURSELF... YOUR FATE IS DESERVEDLY SEALED!
YOU FAT PAIL OF GREASE! I CAN BARELY SQUEEZE YOU THROUGH!
HA- HA- HA- HA- HA- HA--YOU WILL FEED IT--HA- HA- HA-
NO-NO-NO-NO-NO-AHHHHH!!
...EVEN IN DEATH IE FAT FOOL CAUSES BLEMS--NOW I'VE GOT O DISPOSE OF THAT OTHER BODY...
...AHHHHHH-- SLIPPED!
MY BACK-- OH,NO--IT'S--I'M PARALYZED! MY LEGS--I CAN'T MOVE THEM!
I'LL USE MY HANDS-- CRAWL OUT OF HERE AND... OH, LORD, NO! THE DOOR... WHEN I FELL... LOCKED IT... IT... JAMMED SHUT... NO! NO!
...AND THE KEY... IN THERE WITH THAT BUMBLING MORON!

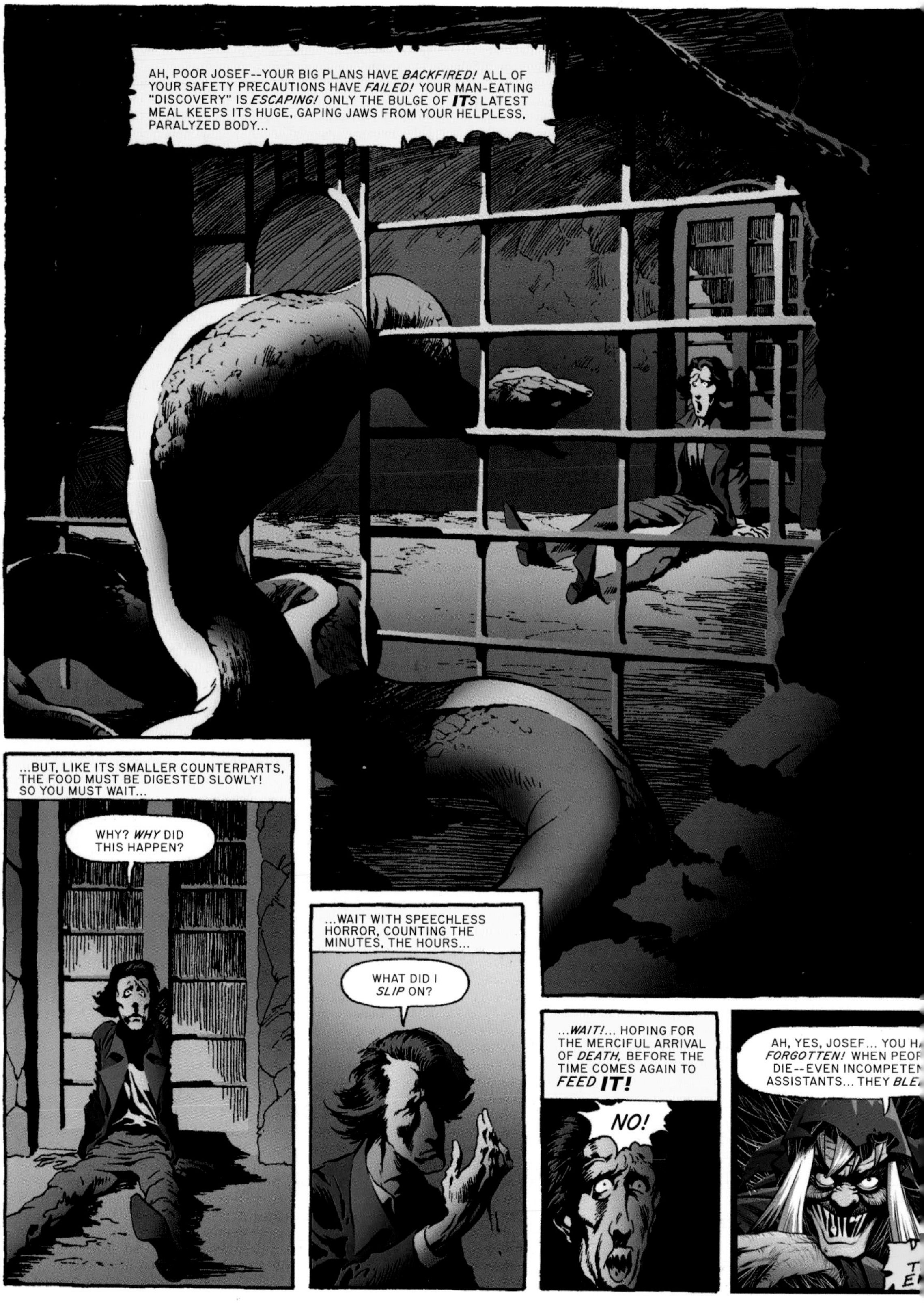
AH, POOR JOSEF--YOUR BIG PLANS HAVE BACKFIRED! ALL OF YOUR SAFETY PRECAUTIONS HAVE FAILED! YOUR MAN-EATING "DISCOVERY" IS ESCAPING! ONLY THE BULGE OF ITS LATEST MEAL KEEPS ITS HUGE, GAPING JAWS FROM YOUR HELPLESS, PARALYZED BODY...
...BUT, LIKE ITS SMALLER COUNTERPARTS, THE FOOD MUST BE DIGESTED SLOWLY! SO YOU MUST WAIT...
WHY? WHY DID THIS HAPPEN?
...WAIT WITH SPEECHLESS HORROR, COUNTING THE MINUTES, THE HOURS...
WHAT DID I SLIP ON?
...WAIT!... HOPING FOR THE MERCIFUL ARRIVAL OF DEATH, BEFORE THE TIME COMES AGAIN TO FEED IT!
NO!
AH, YES, JOSEF... YOU
FORGOTTEN! WHEN
DIE--EVEN
ASSISTANTS... THEY

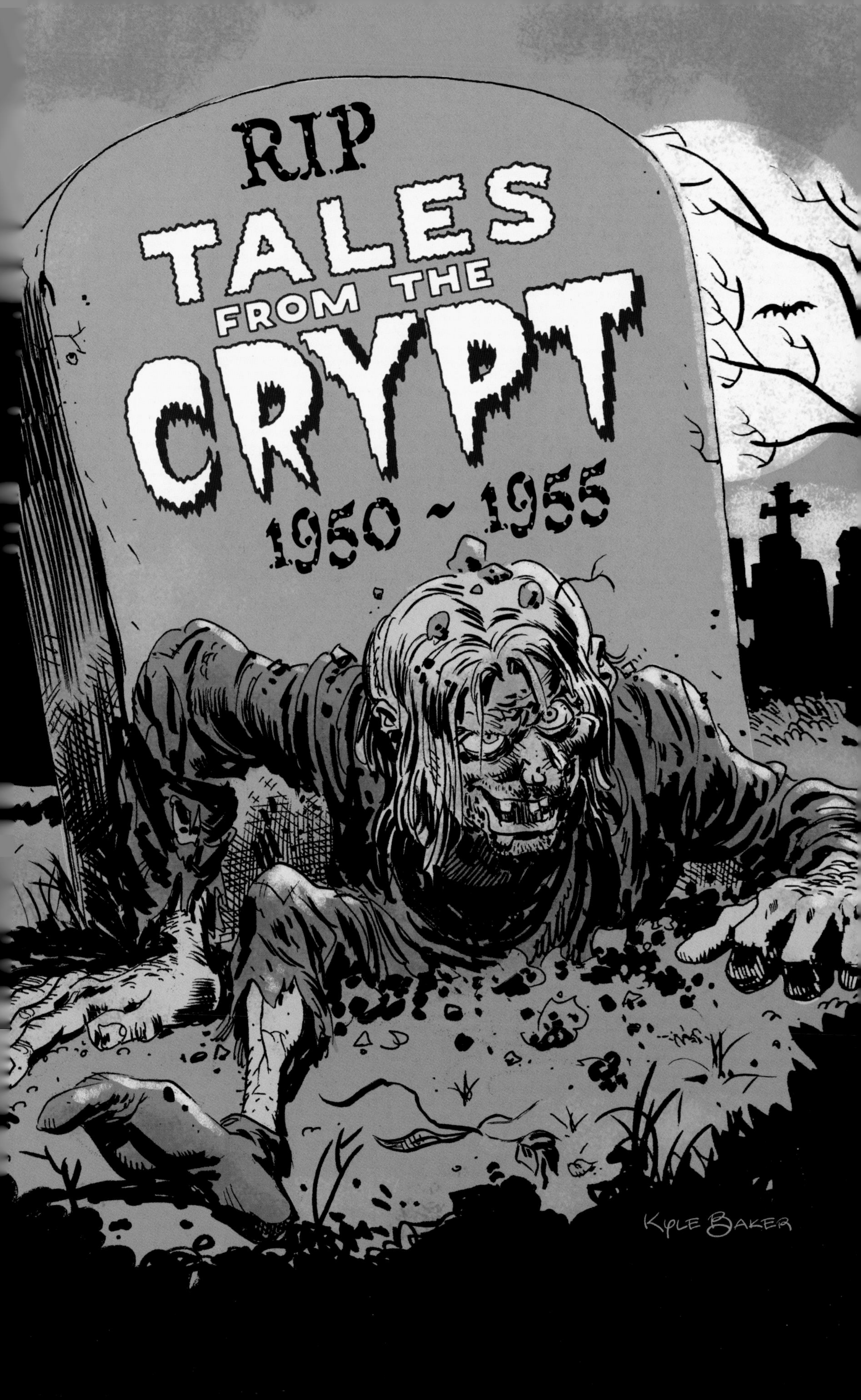
R.I.P.
TALES FROM THE CRYPT
1950 ~ 1955
KYLE BAKER

SUPER GENIUS

TERROR

TALES FROM THE CRYPT®

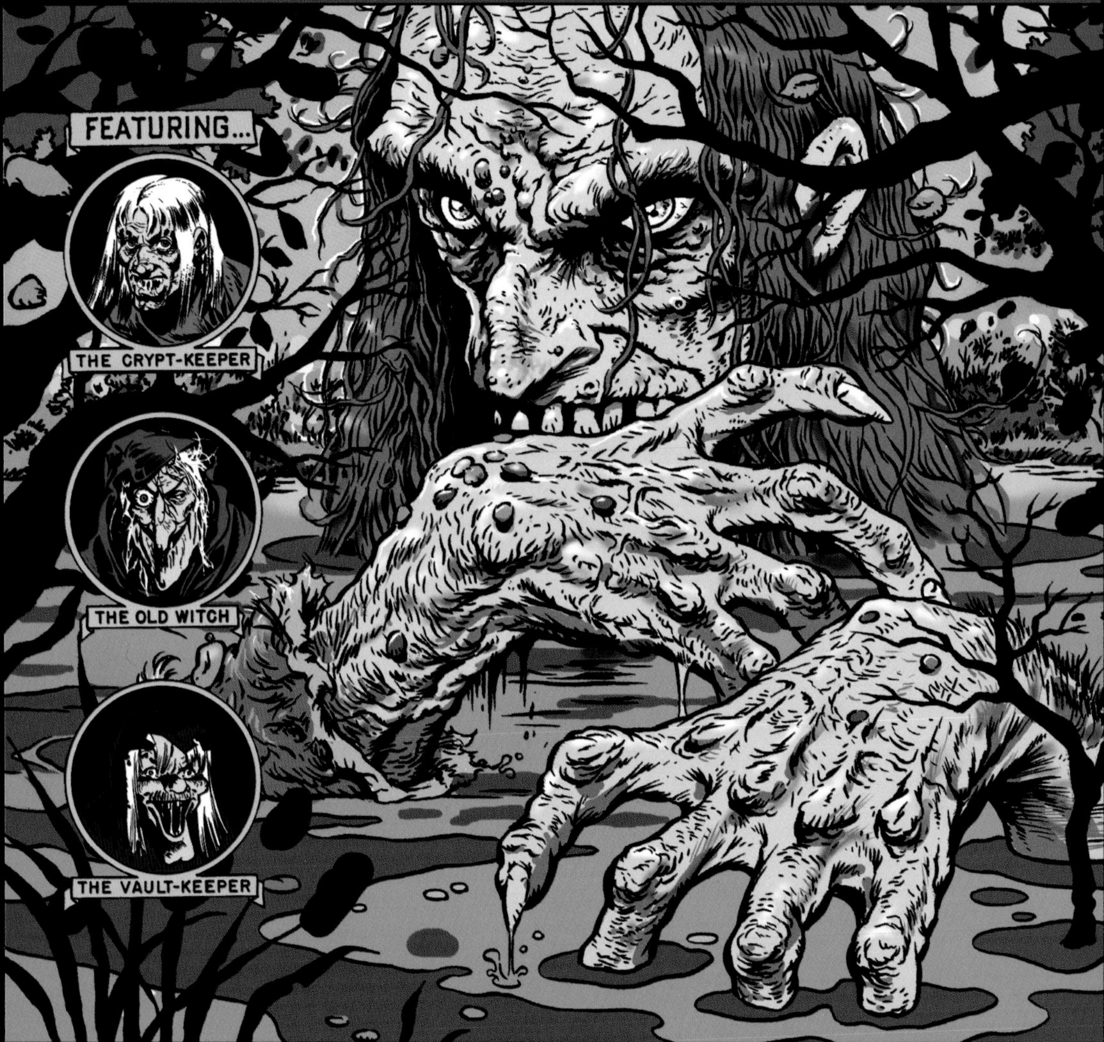
FEATURING...
THE CRYPT-KEEPER
THE OLD WITCH
THE VAULT-KEEPER

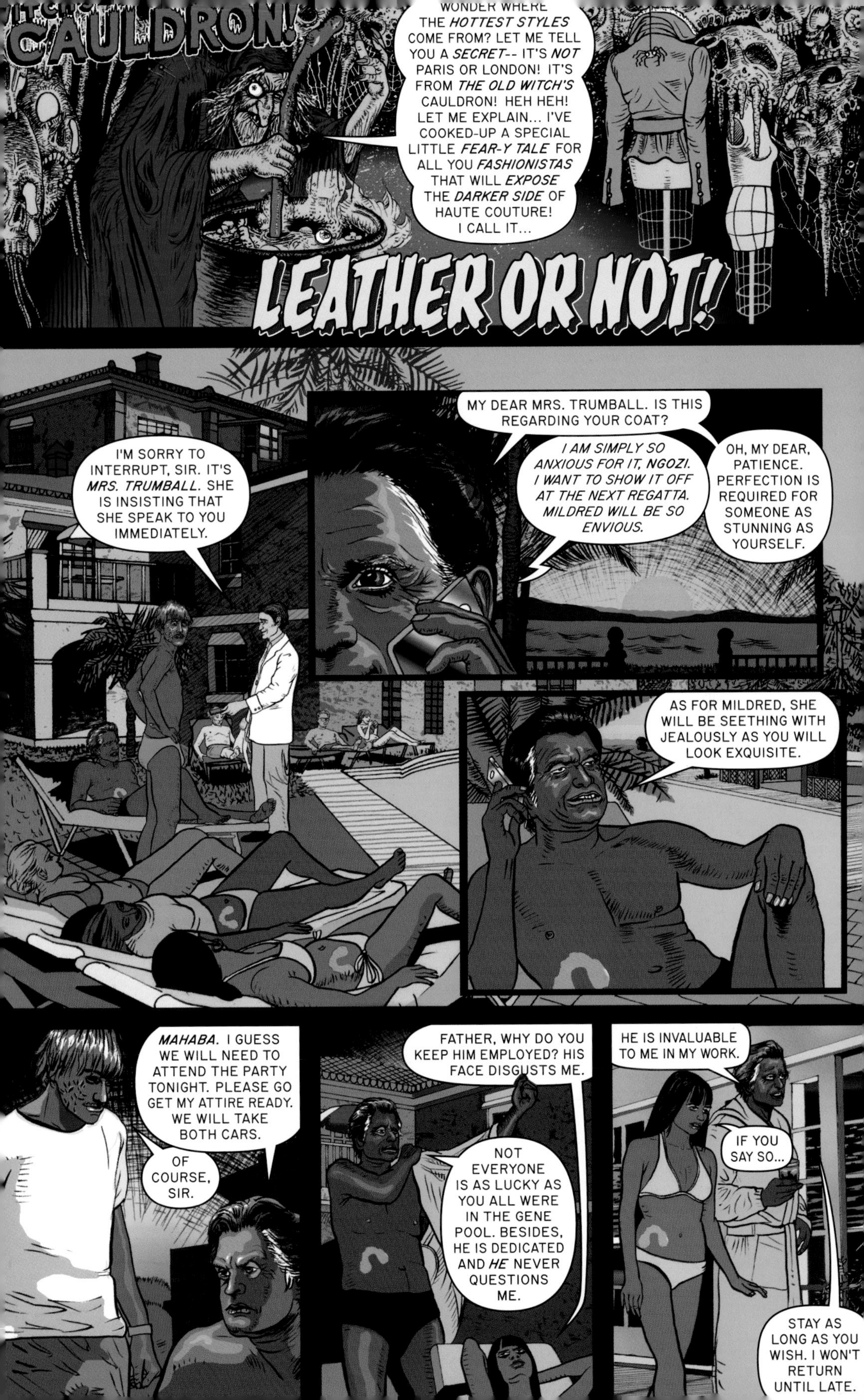

CAULDRON!
WONDER WHERE THE HOTTEST STYLES COME FROM? LET ME TELL YOU A SECRET-- IT'S NOT PARIS OR LONDON! IT'S FROM THE OLD WITCH'S CAULDRON! HEH HEH! LET ME EXPLAIN... I'VE COOKED-UP A SPECIAL LITTLE FEAR-Y TALE FOR ALL YOU FASHIONISTAS THAT WILL EXPOSE THE DARKER SIDE OF HAUTE COUTURE! I CALL IT...
LEATHER OR NOT!
I'M SORRY TO INTERRUPT, SIR. IT'S MRS. TRUMBALL. SHE IS INSISTING THAT SHE SPEAK TO YOU IMMEDIATELY.
MY DEAR MRS. TRUMBALL. IS THIS REGARDING YOUR COAT?
I AM SIMPLY SO ANXIOUS FOR IT, NGOZI. I WANT TO SHOW IT OFF AT THE NEXT REGATTA. MILDRED WILL BE SO ENVIOUS.
OH, MY DEAR, PATIENCE. PERFECTION IS REQUIRED FOR SOMEONE AS STUNNING AS YOURSELF.
AS FOR MILDRED, SHE WILL BE SEETHING WITH JEALOUSLY AS YOU WILL LOOK EXQUISITE.
MAHABA. I GUESS WE WILL NEED TO ATTEND THE PARTY TONIGHT. PLEASE GO GET MY ATTIRE READY. WE WILL TAKE BOTH CARS.
OF COURSE, SIR.
FATHER, WHY DO YOU KEEP HIM EMPLOYED? HIS FACE DISGUSTS ME.
NOT EVERYONE IS AS LUCKY AS YOU ALL WERE IN THE GENE POOL. BESIDES, HE IS DEDICATED AND HE NEVER QUESTIONS ME.
HE IS INVALUABLE TO ME IN MY WORK.
IF YOU SAY SO...
STAY AS LONG AS YOU WISH. I WON'T RETURN UNTIL LATE.

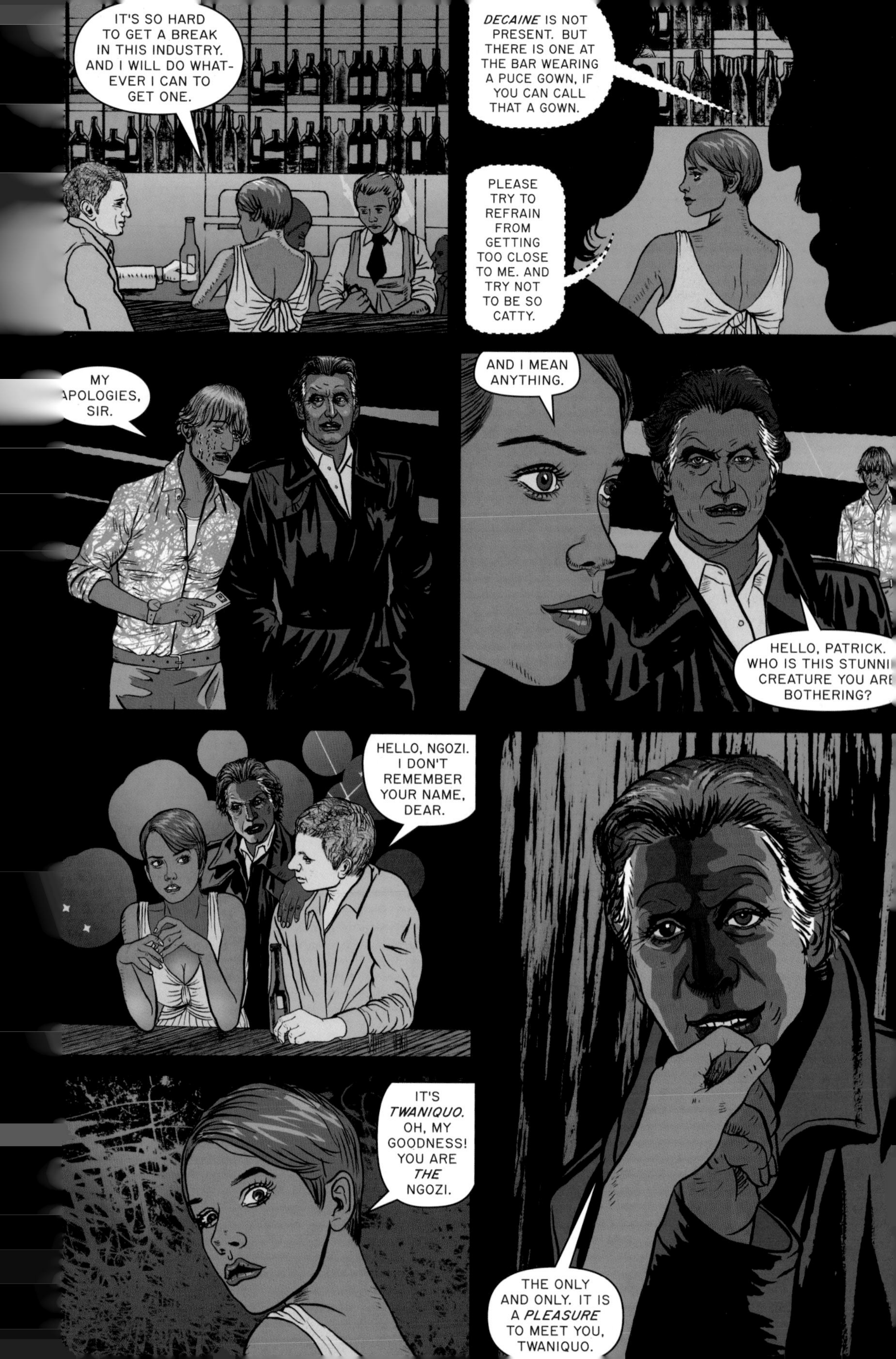
IT'S SO HARD TO GET A BREAK IN THIS INDUSTRY. AND I WILL DO WHAT-EVER I CAN TO GET ONE.
DECAINE IS NOT PRESENT. BUT THERE IS ONE AT THE BAR WEARING A PUCE GOWN, IF YOU CAN CALL THAT A GOWN.
PLEASE TRY TO REFRAIN FROM GETTING TOO CLOSE TO ME. AND TRY NOT TO BE SO CATTY.
MY APOLOGIES, SIR.
AND I MEAN ANYTHING.
HELLO, PATRICK. WHO IS THIS STUNNI CREATURE YOU ARE BOTHERING?
HELLO, NGOZI. I DON'T REMEMBER YOUR NAME, DEAR.
IT'S *TWANIQUO.* OH, MY GOODNESS! YOU ARE *THE* NGOZI.
THE ONLY AND ONLY. IT IS A *PLEASURE* TO MEET YOU, TWANIQUO.

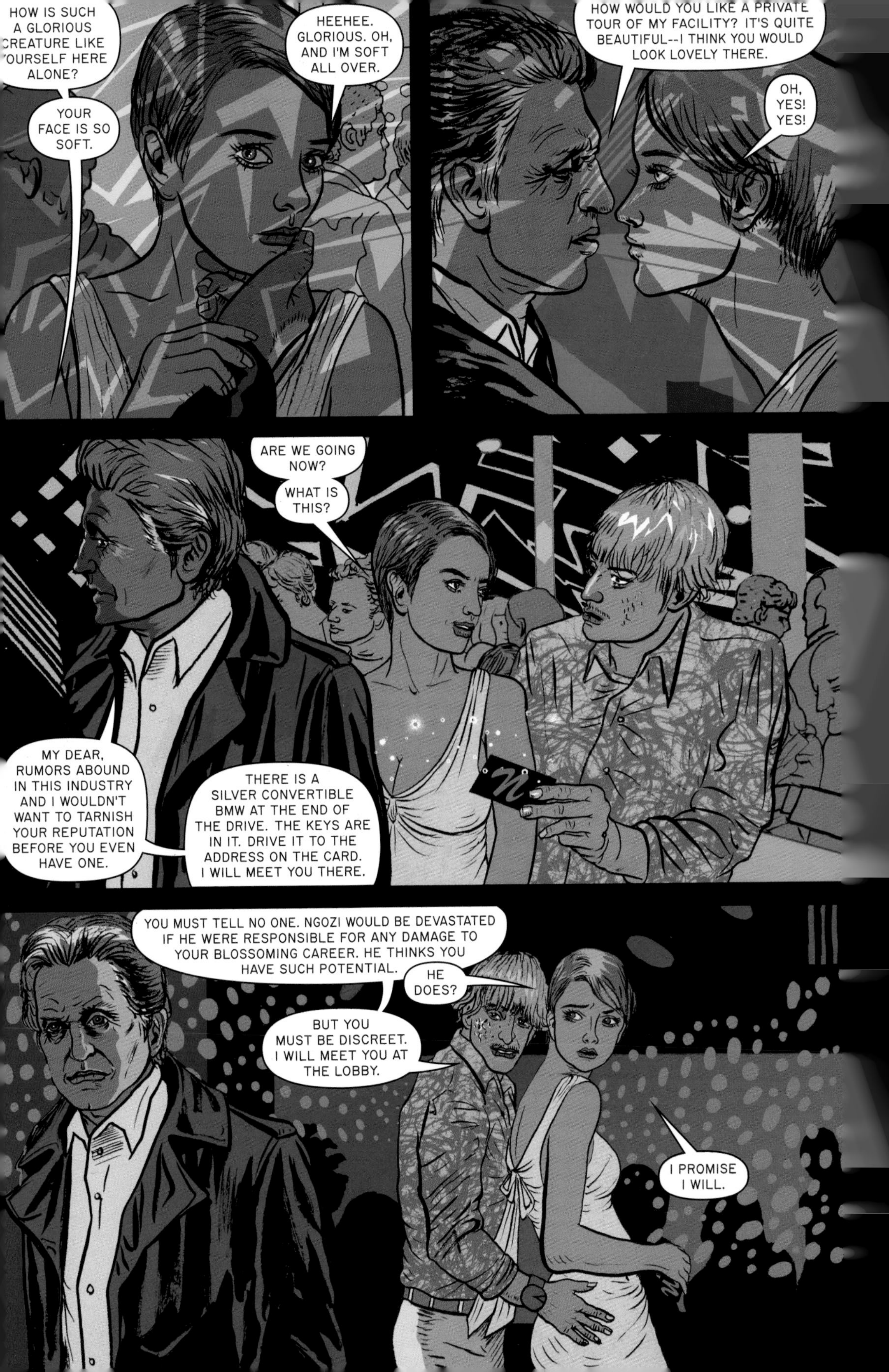
HOW IS SUCH A GLORIOUS CREATURE LIKE YOURSELF HERE ALONE?
YOUR FACE IS SO SOFT.
HEEHEE. GLORIOUS. OH, AND I'M SOFT ALL OVER.
HOW WOULD YOU LIKE A PRIVATE TOUR OF MY FACILITY? IT'S QUITE BEAUTIFUL--I THINK YOU WOULD LOOK LOVELY THERE.
OH, YES! YES!
ARE WE GOING NOW?
WHAT IS THIS?
MY DEAR, RUMORS ABOUND IN THIS INDUSTRY AND I WOULDN'T WANT TO TARNISH YOUR REPUTATION BEFORE YOU EVEN HAVE ONE.
THERE IS A SILVER CONVERTIBLE BMW AT THE END OF THE DRIVE. THE KEYS ARE IN IT. DRIVE IT TO THE ADDRESS ON THE CARD. I WILL MEET YOU THERE.
YOU MUST TELL NO ONE. NGOZI WOULD BE DEVASTATED IF HE WERE RESPONSIBLE FOR ANY DAMAGE TO YOUR BLOSSOMING CAREER. HE THINKS YOU HAVE SUCH POTENTIAL.
HE DOES?
BUT YOU MUST BE DISCREET. I WILL MEET YOU AT THE LOBBY.
I PROMISE I WILL.

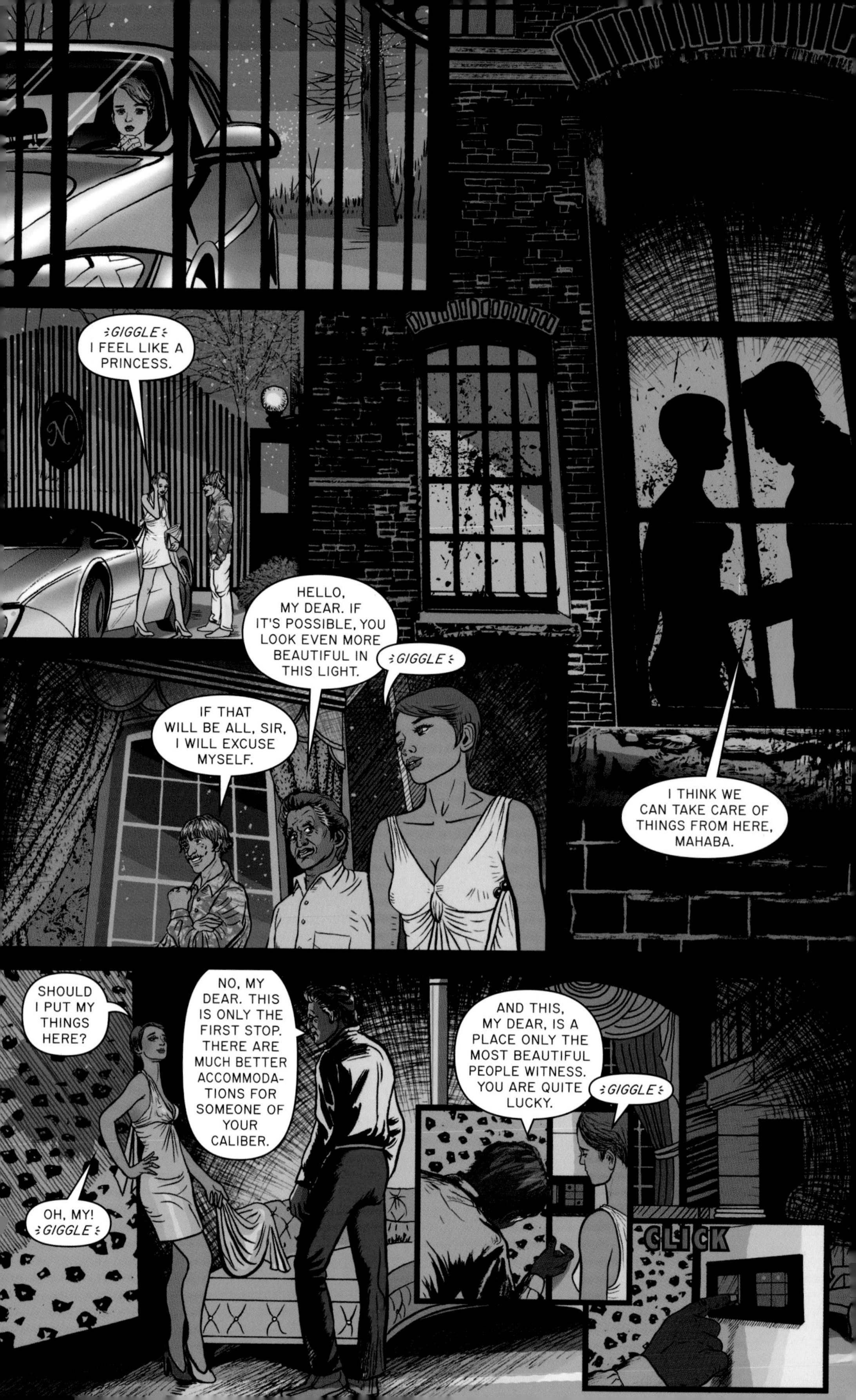
GIGGLE I FEEL LIKE A PRINCESS.
HELLO, MY DEAR. IF IT'S POSSIBLE, YOU LOOK EVEN MORE BEAUTIFUL IN THIS LIGHT.
GIGGLE
IF THAT WILL BE ALL, SIR, I WILL EXCUSE MYSELF.
I THINK WE CAN TAKE CARE OF THINGS FROM HERE, MAHABA.
SHOULD I PUT MY THINGS HERE?
NO, MY DEAR. THIS IS ONLY THE FIRST STOP. THERE ARE MUCH BETTER ACCOMMODATIONS FOR SOMEONE OF YOUR CALIBER.
OH, MY! GIGGLE
AND THIS, MY DEAR, IS A PLACE ONLY THE MOST BEAUTIFUL PEOPLE WITNESS. YOU ARE QUITE LUCKY.
GIGGLE
CLICK

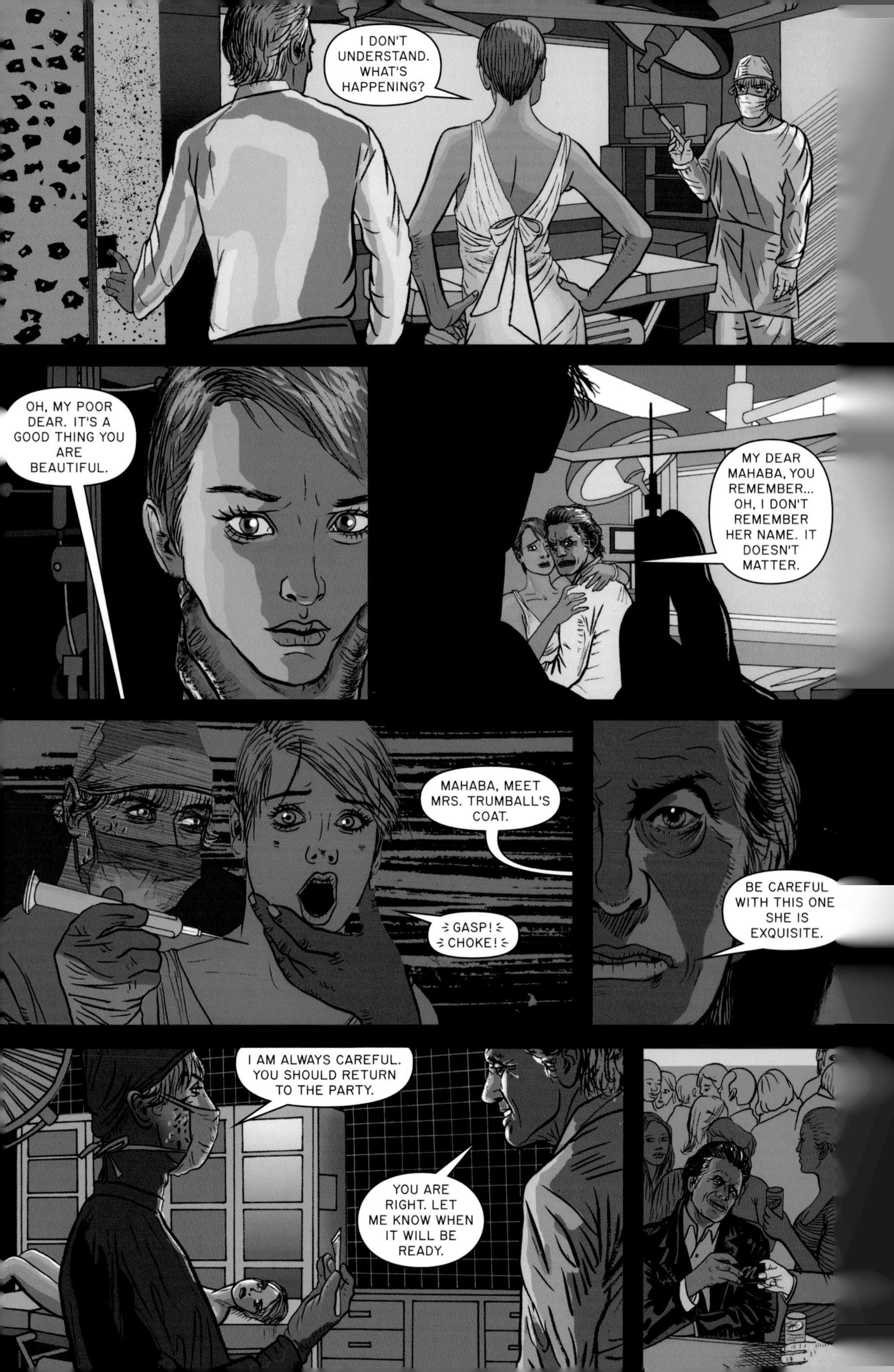
I DON'T UNDERSTAND. WHAT'S HAPPENING?
OH, MY POOR DEAR. IT'S A GOOD THING YOU ARE BEAUTIFUL.
MY DEAR MAHABA, YOU REMEMBER... OH, I DON'T REMEMBER HER NAME. IT DOESN'T MATTER.
MAHABA, MEET MRS. TRUMBALL'S COAT.
GASP! CHOKE!
BE CAREFUL WITH THIS ONE SHE IS EXQUISITE.
I AM ALWAYS CAREFUL. YOU SHOULD RETURN TO THE PARTY.
YOU ARE RIGHT. LET ME KNOW WHEN IT WILL BE READY.

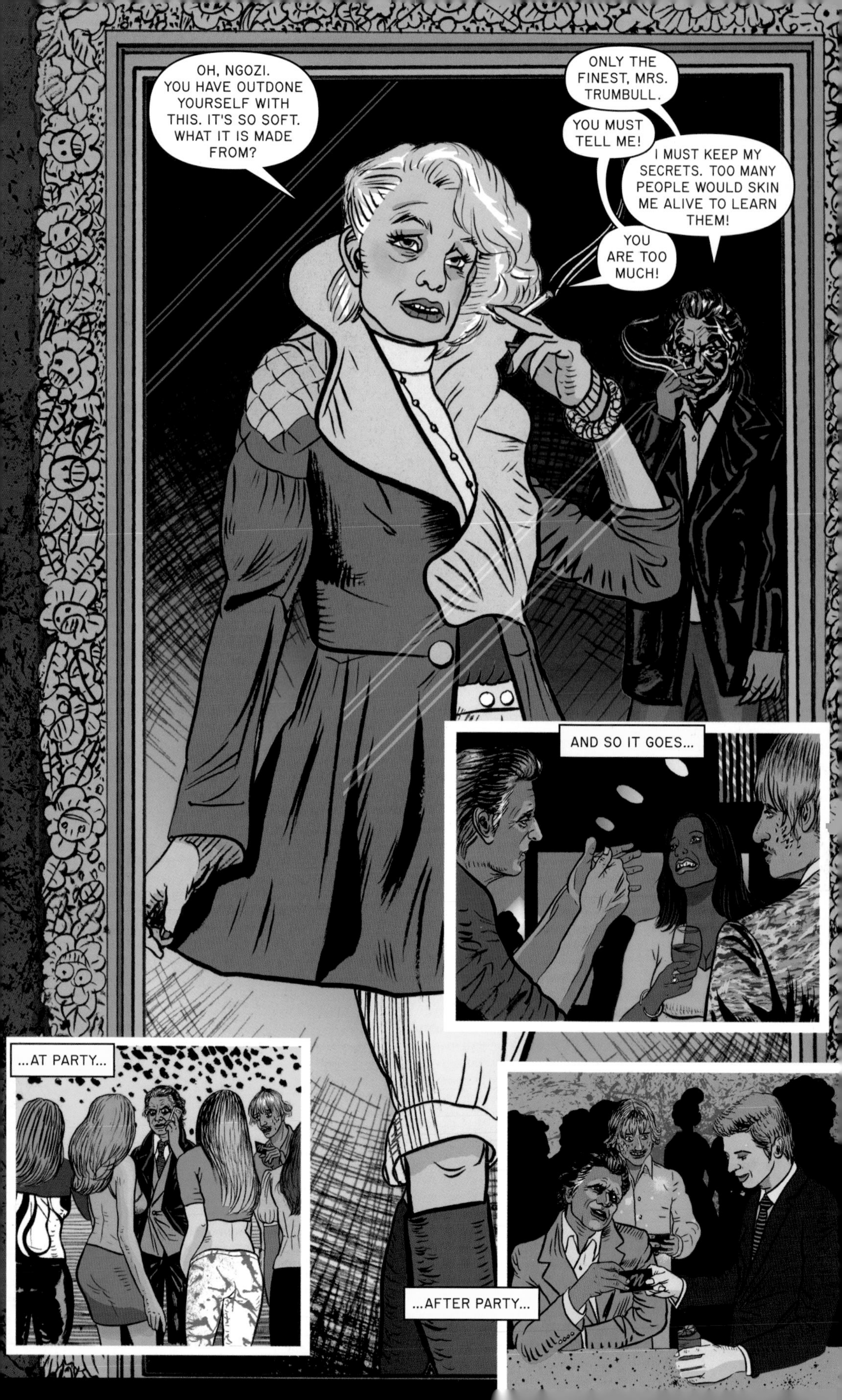
OH, NGOZI. YOU HAVE OUTDONE YOURSELF WITH THIS. IT'S SO SOFT. WHAT IT IS MADE FROM?
ONLY THE FINEST, MRS. TRUMBULL.
YOU MUST TELL ME!
I MUST KEEP MY SECRETS. TOO MANY PEOPLE WOULD SKIN ME ALIVE TO LEARN THEM!
YOU ARE TOO MUCH!
AND SO IT GOES...
...AT PARTY...
...AFTER PARTY...

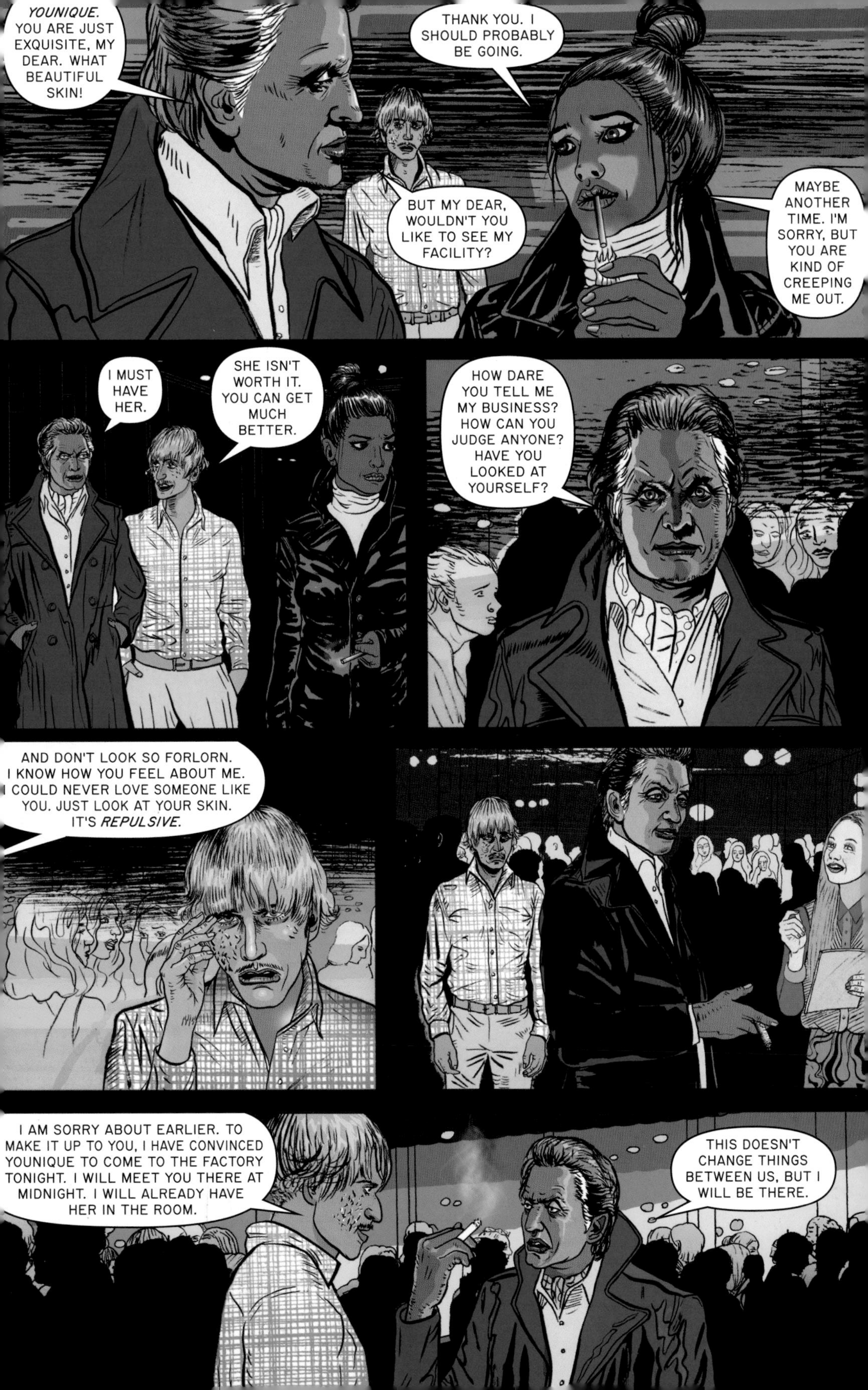
YOUNIQUE. YOU ARE JUST EXQUISITE, MY DEAR. WHAT BEAUTIFUL SKIN!
THANK YOU. I SHOULD PROBABLY BE GOING.
BUT MY DEAR, WOULDN'T YOU LIKE TO SEE MY FACILITY?
MAYBE ANOTHER TIME. I'M SORRY, BUT YOU ARE KIND OF CREEPING ME OUT.
I MUST HAVE HER.
SHE ISN'T WORTH IT. YOU CAN GET MUCH BETTER.
HOW DARE YOU TELL ME MY BUSINESS? HOW CAN YOU JUDGE ANYONE? HAVE YOU LOOKED AT YOURSELF?
AND DON'T LOOK SO FORLORN. I KNOW HOW YOU FEEL ABOUT ME. I COULD NEVER LOVE SOMEONE LIKE YOU. JUST LOOK AT YOUR SKIN. IT'S *REPULSIVE*.
I AM SORRY ABOUT EARLIER. TO MAKE IT UP TO YOU, I HAVE CONVINCED YOUNIQUE TO COME TO THE FACTORY TONIGHT. I WILL MEET YOU THERE AT MIDNIGHT. I WILL ALREADY HAVE HER IN THE ROOM.
THIS DOESN'T CHANGE THINGS BETWEEN US, BUT I WILL BE THERE.

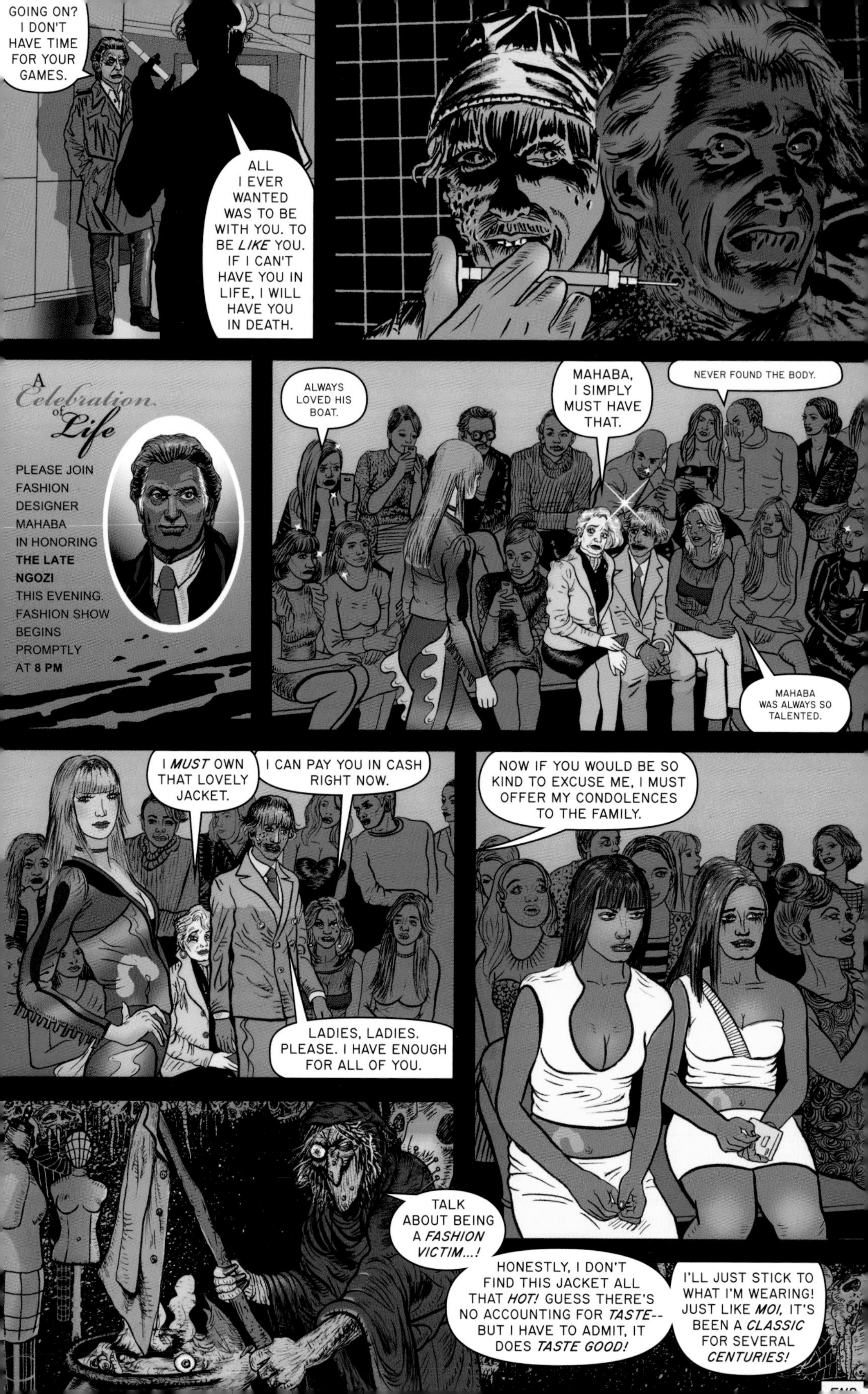
GOING ON? I DON'T HAVE TIME FOR YOUR GAMES.
ALL I EVER WANTED WAS TO BE WITH YOU. TO BE *LIKE* YOU. IF I CAN'T HAVE YOU IN LIFE, I WILL HAVE YOU IN DEATH.
A Celebration of Life
PLEASE JOIN FASHION DESIGNER MAHABA IN HONORING **THE LATE NGOZI** THIS EVENING. FASHION SHOW BEGINS PROMPTLY AT **8 PM**
ALWAYS LOVED HIS BOAT.
MAHABA, I SIMPLY MUST HAVE THAT.
NEVER FOUND THE BODY.
MAHABA WAS ALWAYS SO TALENTED.
I *MUST* OWN THAT LOVELY JACKET.
I CAN PAY YOU IN CASH RIGHT NOW.
LADIES, LADIES. PLEASE. I HAVE ENOUGH FOR ALL OF YOU.
NOW IF YOU WOULD BE SO KIND TO EXCUSE ME, I MUST OFFER MY CONDOLENCES TO THE FAMILY.
TALK ABOUT BEING A *FASHION VICTIM...!*
HONESTLY, I DON'T FIND THIS JACKET ALL THAT *HOT!* GUESS THERE'S NO ACCOUNTING FOR *TASTE*-- BUT I HAVE TO ADMIT, IT DOES *TASTE GOOD!*
I'LL JUST STICK TO WHAT I'M WEARING! JUST LIKE *MOI,* IT'S BEEN A *CLASSIC* FOR SEVERAL *CENTURIES!*